RANDY PATTERSON

THE
MATRIARCH
RULES

RANDY PATTERSON

THE
MATRIARCH
RULES

HOW TO OWN YOUR POWER,
KNOW YOUR WORTH, AND
LEAD THE LIFE YOU'VE
ALWAYS WANTED

WILEY

Published by John Wiley & Sons, Inc., Hoboken, New Jersey.
Published simultaneously in Canada.

For general information on our other products and services or for technical support, please contact our Customer Care Department within the United States at (800) 762-2974, outside the United States at (317) 572-3993 or fax (317) 572-4002.

Wiley publishes in a variety of print and electronic formats and by print-on-demand. Some material included with standard print versions of this book may not be included in e-books or in print-on-demand. If this book refers to media such as a CD or DVD that is not included in the version you purchased, you may download this material at http:// booksupport.wiley.com. For more information about Wiley products, visit www.wiley .com.

Library of Congress Cataloging-in-Publication Data

Names: Patterson, Randy, 1967– author.
Title: The matriarch rules : how to own your power, know your worth, and lead the life you've always wanted / Randy Patterson.
Description: Hoboken, New Jersey : John Wiley & Sons, Inc., [2019] | Includes index. |
Identifiers: LCCN 2019018435 (print) | LCCN 2019020807 (ebook) | ISBN 9781119572725 (Adobe PDF) | ISBN 9781119572718 (ePub) | ISBN 9781119572749 (hardcover)
Subjects: LCSH: Self-realization in women. | Self-esteem in women. | Self-confidence. | Success.
Classification: LCC HQ1206 (ebook) | LCC HQ1206 .P3725 2019 (print) | DDC 155.3/3382—dc23
LC record available at https://lccn.loc.gov/2019018435

Cover Design: Wiley
Photo of author Randy Patterson: © Steve Prue
Background: © noipornpan/iStock.com
Laptop sticker Hudson Valley logo: © Hudson Valley Tattoo Company
Laptop stickers original illustrations: © Tara McPherson

Printed in the United States of America

V10012422_072419

To the Matriarchs who paved the way and set the bar high, Harriet, Marsha, and Janey, I will be forever grateful for your examples of innate wisdom, feminine strength, and familial leadership. You have each impacted my life in immeasurable ways and the legacies you are creating will live on far beyond your years.

To the two women on this earth who truly completed me, my daughters, Erica and Tyler. Your mere presence on this earth has rewarded me in ways I cannot even begin to describe. Thank you forever, my little badasses! I can't wait to one day watch you step into your rightful roles as Matriarchs!

Contents

Acknowledgments   xi

Introduction: Becoming a Modern Matriarch   **1**
    The Modern Matriarch   2
    Loved, but Not Cared For   3
    A Craving for "Normal"   4
    A Truth Moment   5
    When "Wise Counsel" Appears   6
    A Matriarch Today   7

Chapter 1   **The Matriarch Is the CEO**   **9**
    Homeless but Not Helpless   10
    Use Your Resources   12
    Getting on Our Feet   15
    From Baby Blues to Business Partner 16
    Roles and Responsibilities of the
       Matriarch   18

Chapter 2   **A Matriarch's Future Is Based on
       Her Actions Today**   **29**
    Take History-changing Actions   30
    Tally Your Successes and Not Your
       Failures   32
    Write the Story of You: A Woman
       Destined for Great Success   35
    Live Each Day to the Fullest, and Feel
       Like You Absolutely Slayed It   38
    Protect Your Dreams with Your Life!   39

Chapter 3   **The Four Big Lies**   **41**
    Lie #1: I'll Try   43
    Lie #2: I'm Too Busy   45

	Lie #3: I Can't	50
	Lie #4: I Had No Choice	55
Chapter 4	**A Matriarch Owns Her Decisions**	**57**
	Meet Suzie, a Woman in Need of Wise Counsel	59
	The Co-signer: Does She Co-sign Your Agenda or Her Own?	62
	Wise Counsel: She Paints the Big Picture without an Agenda	63
	Confidence Is Key	63
	Decision-making 101	67
Chapter 5	**Attention! We No Longer Work for Free!**	**73**
	We All Want a Bigger, Better Boat and Working for Free Is Not How We'll Get It!	75
	Calling All Matriarchs! Viva la Revolution!	82
Chapter 6	**A Life and Business That's Carefully Crafted**	**93**
	Branding: Just Do It	94
	People Are Their Own Brands	94
	Rebuilding Your Brand Based on Your Authentic Self	97
	Your Brand Aesthetic: Are You Bland or On Brand?	101
	Your Personal Style Guide	104
	Your Family Has Also Been Branded	105
	The Wedding Therapist: Finding the Starting Point for Her Business's Brand	106
	A Carefully Crafted Matriarch Business	108
Chapter 7	**Time Management and the Five Rules of Business**	**113**
	Time Management	114
	Let's Go Make Some Money, Matriarch!	117

Rule #1: It Starts with a Plan   119
Rule #2: It's Got to Be Legal   121
Rule #3: It Takes a Systematic Approach   123
Rule #4: Marketing Is a Never-ending
    Process   124
Rule #5: You've Got to Be Found on
    the Web   126
Manage Your Time and Follow the
    Rules   128

Chapter 8   **The Payoff Is Personal**   **131**
Confidence Can Overcome an Old
    Message   131
Confidence, Meet Systems and Tools   133
Passion: A Strong and Barely
    Controllable Emotion   134
Inspiration and Motivation   137
Maintaining Motivation   140
Pressure Is How Diamonds Are Made   142
A Matriarch Maintains and Protects
    What She Builds   143
Make NOT Having These F.E.A.R.S.
    Your Biggest Fears   144

Chapter 9   **A Matriarch Leaves a Great Legacy**   **147**
What Exactly Is a Legacy?   148
Leaving a Legacy Whether You Like It
    or Not ...   148
My Mom, Shari ...   149
A Matriarch Lives an Intentional Life   150
A Matriarch Cultivates an Inner
    Sanctum   151
A Matriarch Gives and Takes   152
A Matriarch Rocks Out to Her Own
    Soundtrack   153
A Matriarch Knows Her Language Is
    Her Legacy   154

A Matriarch Switches Gears When
Necessary   155
Live Like a Matriarch and Leave a
Legacy Worthy of a Matriarch!   156

About the Author   **159**

Index   **161**

Acknowledgments

To my book-writing "wise counsel," Jenni and Vicki, thank you so much for your support and guidance throughout this amazingly rewarding process!

Introduction

Becoming a Modern Matriarch

I was 12 years old, my hair was too curly, my glasses were too big, and my self-esteem was too low. I walked in the door after school one day and my mom said, "You're babysitting for the neighbors' kids tonight." "I am? How much will they pay me?" "We didn't discuss that. You'll get whatever she gives you."

And so it began. My services had whatever value the person receiving them decided on ... The lesson? Asking for money is wrong, rude, and presumptuous. Can you relate?

The best way to describe the effects of this is by saying life just happens to you; you get what you get, and you shouldn't expect more. This set me up for a world where accepting what I was given became the norm.

My mother was telling me what I was going to do, and I understood perfectly. She had the power to control me, and for some reason, she was more concerned about the lady who needed a babysitter than about teaching me the life lesson of charging my worth.

Message downloaded and saved to my hard drive as my_inner_voice.pdf.

This was the set up for many years of lying to myself about my worth and building and collecting evidence that supported those lies. In fact, I built and collected so much evidence that I became personally bankrupt. I had no self-esteem and no opinion about anything.

Someone would say, "What do you want to do?" I'd say, "Whatever you want to do is good." They'd ask, "What do you want for dinner?" "Whatever you want is fine." The same happened when it came to watching a movie, listening to music, and basically any other decision a human being would encounter on their journey through life.

Now, the problem with this is that with no self-esteem and no opinion, you can easily find yourself in situations that quickly escalate beyond your control. Situations that contribute to that low self-esteem and more evidence of your unworthiness. This is how we find ourselves fat, in debt, in bad relationships, in jobs we hate, screaming at our kids, and so on and so forth. Leaving us feeling guilty, powerless, stuck, without choices, and flat out miserable.

So this was me. A defeated, helpless, hopeless, seemingly unlovable rag of a girl. I didn't know I had any power and I was freely giving it away to anyone who would take it. But I could spot a woman who knew she had power a mile away. For one thing, I could tell she was in charge the second she walked into a room. She was bold. She was fierce, and she had her own unique style. When she smiled, she wasn't worried if there was food stuck in her teeth. And so what if there was? She knew that something that insignificant couldn't define her.

I needed to become this. Eventually, I did. And now, I'm going to show you how to do the same.

The Modern Matriarch

Throughout my adult life I have defined this woman as a Matriarch. A Matriarch is a female head of the family or tribal line, a woman who is the founder or dominant member of a community or group, a venerable woman – someone commanding respect or reverence.

The Matriarch isn't some crusty old lady dressed head-to-toe in black who sits at the head of the table barking demands at Sunday dinner. The modern Matriarch is alive and vivacious. She's purposeful and deliberate about everything, from her career, to her home, to her family, to what she eats for lunch.

She does not second guess herself but moves herself and those she loves boldly toward the future.

If a Matriarch has children, they are a major focus of her life. She will fight to the death for her family, and her kids know that having her as their mom is like winning the life lottery. Career and professional success matter to her too. Her vision for her career is as big as her love for her family, and she's paid her worth for the work that she's passionate about. She wouldn't have it any other way. A Matriarch knows exactly what she wants the end game to be and she knows she has the power to make it come to fruition. A Matriarch has her shit together and you feel safer and more secure when you're in her presence. She doesn't try to be this person – she IS this person. Long before I ever imagined myself in this role, I knew I wanted it.

Loved, but Not Cared For

The household I grew up in looked very different than the one I created for myself. My parents lived in self-will. They had an "if it feels good, do it" attitude. Drugs felt good. Overeating felt good. Taking advantage of the system felt good. Walking into a store and leaving with something you didn't pay for felt good. The lights were dim, the curtains were drawn, the garbage spilled over, and doing dishes never seemed a priority. We collected welfare and ate from food stamps and if shame was attached to it, they never let on.

I was loved, but not cared for, and there's a big difference between the two. When you're not cared for, you become really comfortable settling for whatever you get. Again, it's as if life is happening to you rather than you making life happen for you. So it's not surprising that I grew up with zero self-esteem and initially made some really crappy choices. I took comfort in drugs and alcohol; I dropped out of high school in 11th grade, held a series of go-nowhere jobs, and eventually found myself desperate and homeless. Not exactly a recipe for success.

My life and self-esteem were not intact, but even at my lowest, I knew there was a path to success, and I was determined to find it. I craved a "normal" family and a clean home. I wanted parents who upheld traditions and worked hard for what they wanted in life – not parents who would ask me to "go see if the neighbor's lights were off too" when the power went out.

A Craving for "Normal"

Glimpses of "normal" would entice me to fantasize about a future life where I was in the driver's seat. It was usually after a visit to my aunt's house in New Jersey. Picture this: I'm 13 years old, and I live in New York. Now keep in mind, this was long before anyone had a cell phone. I would leave my house with a small packed suitcase (without wheels), walk into town, and wait at the bus stop. The bus would arrive, and I would ask the driver if this bus went to New Jersey. He would say yes, and I'd climb the three steps onto the bus while schlepping my luggage awkwardly beside me. I would make my way to a seat and stare out the window while all that was familiar to me disappeared. About an hour later, the bus driver would let me know that I had arrived at my stop. After doing this a couple of times, I learned to walk to my aunt's house from the bus stop unassisted.

Now this all sounds pretty gnarly, right? A kid traveling by themselves with no support or protection ... But let me tell you, these trips to my aunt's house were so worth the risk. They inspired much more in me than I could ever tell you in this book.

At my aunt's house is where NORMAL PEOPLE lived. There were three cousins. The older brother cousin was the All-American boy. He was a great student, an amazing athlete, and quite the lady's man. Then there were the twin sister cousins who were just a few years older than me. They were everything I ever wanted to be. They both had jobs at the Ice Cream Station and used the money to buy their own school clothes. Their bedroom was immaculate. It was huge. It was beautifully decorated. And they made their beds every day. Everyday! Can you imagine?

One time, while I was visiting my aunt and uncle, they were redecorating the dining room of their beautiful home. I was in awe. My aunt had chosen the most gorgeous wallpaper I had ever seen. If I remember correctly, it was silver flocked with black raised-crushed velvet fleurs-de-lis. It was magnificent. As my uncle applied the paper, I imagined my aunt in the store looking at samples and choosing the one that would wrap the walls where her family would come together for meals, holidays, and celebrations. I was blown away by watching this woman, my aunt, creating an environment so deliberately and with such leadership.

The family I was born into lacked leadership. There was no responsible adult making decisions about anything – money, meals, chores, holidays, school – and we all suffered as a result.

A Truth Moment

When I decided I wanted to drop out of high school, the deal my mom offered was, have a full-time job within one week and, in return, she would sign the papers required by the school to allow me to quit. Within 24 hours, I convinced the manager at 5 Star Value, a total shithole bargain basement closeout store, that I could price cat food and cans of soup better and faster than anyone he'd ever seen. And just like that, I got the full-time job that represented my freedom from high school.

I hitchhiked to 5 Star Value every day with both sides of my head shaved, too much black eyeliner on, and the biggest "fuck you" attitude I could muster. But here's what you should know. When my inner rage wasn't overshadowing everything else, I'd hear this quiet voice, deep inside me, that simply whispered, "You can do better." And each time I heard it, I cranked up the volume on the heaviest, loudest, raunchiest heavy metal I could get my hands on to drown it out.

I had these moments of clarity, as fleeting as they were, and one of the most profound happened on a day when I got up for work and just before leaving the house, I reached into the couch cushions looking for $1.25. That's how much a slice of pizza and a Coke were, and I was planning ahead for my lunch break. So as 12:30 rolled around, I clocked out and walked next door to the pizzeria. I asked the guy for a slice and a Coke, and

I waited a couple of minutes while he heated it up. He handed me a bent red plastic tray with a paper plate and a greasy slice of pizza on it and a can of Coke that almost slid off the tray as I turned to walk away.

I stopped and I steadied it, and out of the corner of my eye, on the counter, I saw a tray of condiments: salt, pepper, garlic powder, parmesan cheese, and red pepper flakes. And I thought to myself, "Damn it! I get to have that! It's available to me and I get to have it." I walked over, put my tray down, and began covering my slice with every condiment available. Now mind you, I didn't even like that stuff, but I wanted what I could have, and the thought occurred to me briefly that the world had tons of shit to offer; I just had to step up and go get it.

That day could have been a turning point for me. I could have grabbed hold of that truth and begun to climb out of those dark days. How many people have repeatedly found themselves in these truth moments, but ignored them like I did, and just turned up the music? How many people have stood on the precipice of these life-altering opportunities and rather than saying, "Yes, I can" to them have said, "No, I'm not worthy" and have dived deeper into the darkness.

I stood there in that truth moment, paused, and then said to myself, *Bitch, you hitchhiked here, you work at 5 Star Value, and you dug in the couch cushion for lunch money ...*

Those may have been the facts, but they certainly weren't the truth. Regardless, I bought that lie for a buck twenty-five.

When "Wise Counsel" Appears

For the next handful of years I was a thrill seeker. I wanted to party, and I wanted to dull the pain of low self-esteem. In the end, it all added up to a one-way ticket to rehab in California, and that's where I met Monica. Monica was just a few years older than me and she was my counselor. She was a woman in charge, and she recognized the badass in me. It made her laugh and it made me feel good.

Monica was investing in me. She was investing in me in a way that no one ever had before, and it contributed to my self-worth. Since Monica thought that I had value, and I valued Monica, I had no choice but to start believing her. Monica was the first person in my life to offer me what I now refer to as "wise counsel."

One day, she gave me an assignment. She told me that that night, before I went to bed, I had to write a "Self-Esteem List." She challenged me to write a list of three things that I liked about myself. Her only instruction was that I couldn't write things like "I have nice hair" or "pretty eyes."

Because it was Monica, and I felt like she genuinely liked me and wanted me to succeed, I gave it a whirl. I got a pen and a notebook. I got into bed, opened to a clean sheet of paper, clicked the pen and ... nothing. I gave it a minute. I started to think to myself, there must be something. A moment later ... still nothing. Maybe if I put the pen on the paper, something would come. Nothing. I got mad. I felt defeated. The rage in me exploded. I wrote one word and closed the notebook. The word was written with such force that it penetrated nearly a dozen pages beneath it. The word was *F U C K*.

Day two was a repeat of day one – nothing. By day three I was getting desperate. That's when I decided that I would start living purposefully. That I would live like I had to make a list at the end of the day. I didn't exactly change the world with my actions, but I wrote about how I made someone laugh. I wrote about how I was the kind of person who can give a genuine compliment. I wrote about how I told someone that her voice was soothing and it made her happy.

And for the first time in a long time, I fell asleep feeling worthy. It started with a decision. A heavy, hard-to-make decision that changed absolutely everything.

A Matriarch Today

Fast forward 30 years. I am a Matriarch. I am a venerable woman. I am a loving and devoted wife and the mother of two unbelievably badass adult daughters; I am the co-founder and CEO of a million-dollar start-up; I have achieved personal and professional success in numerous ways; and ultimately, I am happy and proud of my accomplishments.

I am going to take you on the journey of how I went from a powerless and shattered girl to an empowered and vivacious business woman, wife, and mother. My friends: The road was well traveled. It was windy; it was mostly uphill; it was usually raining; and it sucked. I'll tell you about the period where I lived outside because I didn't have a home. I'll tell you how I set small goals and worked every day to achieve them. And I'll tell you how I treated every setback as a setup for a comeback.

I'm confident that as I take you on this journey with me, in the bushes or in the trees, on the sidewalks or in the ditches, you will see a glimpse of yourself, and you will find hope. From there, I will equip you with the mind-sets to make your own life-altering decisions.

But first, my challenge to you right now is to create a picture of who and where you want to be. And then I'll show you how to get there.

Matriarch Must-Do #1

Start a Self-Esteem List. Before you close your eyes at the end of this day, write a list of three things you like about yourself.

Matriarch Must-Do #2

Take whatever time you need to answer these questions:

1. What do I want?
2. How can I get it?
3. What is my end goal?

Chapter 1

The Matriarch Is the CEO

I had created my first good habit. Each night before I went to bed, I wrote that list of things I liked about myself. What started with a search for three simple behaviors had grown to a list of 10, and then 15, and then 20, and so on. I began writing with confidence as I became more and more accountable for how I lived my life and, low and behold, my self-esteem began to grow. What's interesting is that as my self-esteem increased, I found that I was becoming more and more dissatisfied with settling for whatever life threw my way. I think what I was experiencing was called self-worth, and I, Randy Patterson, was becoming increasingly more worthy by the day.

But what is most important in this life lesson, and what I'm begging you to hear, is that I, me, just me, is what changed things. The power had been within me all along, but no external source could ignite it until I decided it was time. Somehow, with a tiny bit of support, I became ready and decided the time was now. Monica may have told me to write a list, but she didn't write it, and she had no power to get me to do it. She just seemed to care. And that was what I needed to get ready enough to do it. Now, you may think that you don't have a Monica, but that's just another lie you tell yourself so you can remain convinced that you suck.

You have a Monica. I am *your* Monica. And YOU don't suck!

For me, the momentum really started to build when I began asking myself the very same questions that I just asked you.

1. What do I want?
2. How can I get it?
3. What is my end goal?

These may sound simple, but it was just the very beginning. No one had ever asked me these questions before; I had not asked them of myself; and no one had ever worked to help me find or nurture my desires. On a side note, a Matriarch asks these questions of her people and she fosters their ideas.

But I'm getting ahead of myself. Come with me back to San Diego, California ...

Homeless but Not Helpless

At the time, I was in my early 20s and in a relationship with my now husband, Jerry Patterson. Our living situation was crumbling before our eyes. We'd been living with some friends and probably not pulling our weight. We did, however, get out of the house every week to pick up a free block of cheese, some powdered milk, and a bucket of peanut butter that was offered by the community center. We called this our "contribution to the household," but I guess it wasn't enough "rent" for two adults sharing their home, electricity, water, and furnishings. They were gently but firmly saying, the buck stops here, it's time for you guys to move on.

And just like that, our address became San Diego, California. We were officially homeless.

My parents lived in an apartment in the area, and when we turned to them for shelter, well, let's just say ... it didn't go so well. They believed that allowing us to crash with them would be a form of "enabling" us, and suddenly, after 22 years of parenting me, they became concerned with how their decisions would impact my life ... Now, of all fucking times?!

They did, however, allow us to come over, have a shower, and grab a bite to eat. I remember my mom saying it was time for us to go and getting absolutely furious. I knew if I lost my shit and freaked out on her she wouldn't change her mind, so I tried a different strategy. I thought if I could get her alone, I might be able to convince her that we should stay.

I sarcastically said, "Do you have a roll of toilet paper we can take with us in case one of us has to take a shit?" She nodded and I followed her into the bathroom. Once we were alone, our eyes locked and I said, "Ya know, Mom, we're both gonna cry ourselves to sleep tonight, only I'm gonna know where you are ..."

Well, that was it. Like the woman had fire raging through her veins and salivary glands full of venom, she looked deep into my eyes and said, "Get the fuck out and don't let the door hit you in the ass!"

So we left.

We had two sleeping bags, an acoustic guitar, a garbage bag filled with clothes, and a battery-operated alarm clock – and off we went. The first thing we needed to do was find a place to sleep. As we walked out of their apartment, we noticed that the parking lot had a numbered spot with a covered carport and an elevated storage bin for each unit. We searched until we found a vacant one and Jerry threw our stuff up into the storage bin. The "bin" was a long cabinet that was about 8 to 10 feet long and about 3 feet deep. Jerry cupped his hands and locked his fingers which was the signal for me to step in so he could hoist me up and I could climb in. Once I was up there, I unrolled the sleeping bags and placed them longways so we could lay head to head. There was actually something kind of cool about this, but make no mistake, this was not a permanent solution.

The mornings passed and they certainly posed their challenges. As car doors opened and ignitions turned over, I was terrified that we'd be found. The scramble of tenants opening and closing car doors and heading off to work seemed to go on for hours each day. I was sure we'd be busted and made to leave.

Each day, when it quieted down, Jerry would peek out, announce that the coast was clear, and we'd hop down. We would shut the double doors behind us, leaving our belongings inside. Next, we'd find a gas station within walking distance to pee, brush our teeth, and give ourselves a sink bath.

P.S. Most outside gas station bathrooms don't have hot water.

At that point in my life, the answers to the three questions above were:

1. To live inside.
2. By making money.
3. To have a sense of security.

And that's when I added a fourth question:

4. What steps will I take to achieve it?

Use Your Resources

Step 1 was to get a job.

Some weeks went by, and Jerry found himself on a construction crew as a day laborer carrying lumber and boxes of nails, and I decided I'd apply for a job at the snack bar in the bowling alley. That's when it dawned on me. They'd want me to fill out an application, and the application would ask for my phone number and address ... neither of which I had. Feeling defeated, I walked. Eyes down, feet shuffling, mind racing, I walked as negative thoughts flooded my mind.

And then, out of nowhere, a quiet voice inside me whispered, *Be resourceful.*

I looked up and to my left was the dilapidated Vista Riviera Motel. The Vista Riviera was synonymous with drug dealing, hourly room-renting prostitutes, and bleary-eyed dope fiends. But somehow, through my lens, I saw an opportunity. Outside the front office was a woman I knew briefly. She smiled and waved, and I found myself walking toward her. I don't even know why. It just started happening and I didn't stop it.

I asked her if they were hiring, as if I knew anything about working at a motel. I said I could do anything they needed, and I told her I was desperate for work. She said they weren't hiring and that they could barely afford to pay the people who cleaned the rooms. That's when, the "Be resourceful voice" started screaming! It said, *Tell her you'll clean the rooms in exchange for one to live in!* And just like that, we had a place to live.

Step 2 was to find a less disgusting, more permanent place to live, that wasn't infested with cockroaches and didn't have drunken assholes banging on doors at 3 a.m.

We knew that to accomplish that it would take money – way more than we had. And while cleaning those rooms offered us a place to lay our heads at night, I wasn't earning a paycheck. After my morning cleaning duties at the motel one day, I walked over to the bowling alley. I opened the door, and a couple of minutes later, I was standing in front of the snack bar. With all of the courage I could muster, I asked the young girl at the counter if they were hiring. She said she wasn't sure and told me that the manager had just left but that I could fill out an application and she would get it to him. I said, "Nah, that's cool. I'll just come back when he's in. Do you know when he'll be back?"

She said he was there most days, but his schedule was kind of random. And so it began. I went to the bowling alley every day at different times and asked if he was in. Each day, the young girl said no and tried to get me to fill out that fucking application. And each day, I refused. By the sixth or seventh day, I walked in and she said, "He's here! The manager is here. I'll get him."

The dude comes out and says, "You really want to work at the snack bar, huh? They say you come here every day trying to get a job." In that moment, I could hardly even remember why I wanted that particular job so badly. I mean, I could walk there, so that was good. And I imagined it wouldn't be too difficult to learn how to flip a hamburger, so that was a plus. But it really did seem like I was unusually obsessed with getting this job. At any rate, I was hired, and I started the next day.

Payday was on Friday but check this shit out … they held back your first week's pay! Talk about kickin' you while you're down. We had nothing, and now I had to work for two weeks before they'd pay me a dime. Clearly, it's normal for your first week's pay to be held back, but at the time, it felt like another opportunity for life to slap me in the face and show me how fucked I was.

The second Friday came along, and they handed me my measly minimum wage, part-time paycheck. And then it occurred to me. How will I cash this check with no bank account?! I live in a roach motel, and the "fine establishment" was not a permanent address for opening a bank account.

A friend told me about something called a "check-cashing" place. You go in, wait in line at a bullet proof glass window, and when it's your turn, you slip your check and ID through the opening in the glass and they hand you the cash! Great, right?! Nope! These assholes take 10% of your check as a service fee and you leave feeling like you've been kicked in the teeth and handed a bag to put them in. To say things were hard was an understatement, and I often wonder what kept us going.

Week after week, we walked to the check-cashing place on Fridays and took what they gave us. We worked hard, spent little, and stockpiled every dollar in a brown paper bag that we kept under the bathroom sink in our roach room. Eventually, we had a decent little pile and began looking for the cheapest apartment we could find. We found a one-bedroom apartment not too far away, slapped down a security deposit and the first month's rent, and made 508 N. Citrus Ave., Vista, California, our very own address!

Goal achieved.

The following week we bought a chair at the Salvation Army for $2.50 and we took turns sitting on it while eating spaghetti, kielbasa, or beans and rice for dinner. It was all ours and we were so proud! This would be the very first life event that qualified for what I now call my "I Don't Suck List." This list is a compilation of evidence that reminds me that I am capable. When I stand at a crossroads where life feels hard, where I feel like I'm failing, where I am not sure if I can handle what's coming next, I whip out my "I Don't Suck List." One glance at this personal inventory and I am reminded of exactly how much I am capable of.

Matriarch Must-Do #3

Start your "I Don't Suck List" now!

Getting on Our Feet

From the time I was 17 years old, working at my parents record store in Warwick, New York, and Jerry Patterson walked in, all I ever wanted to be was his wife and the mother of his children. Oh, that perfect combination of tight jeans, high top sneakers, long flowing hair, and punk rock attitude: I was hooked. I couldn't get enough of him. He asked for my number and I hoped he'd call. This was back in 1983, long before the days of creeping on someone's social media, so I just waited and, sure enough, he called.

And that's where our love story began. We were kids but it felt like we were life partners, soul mates. We lived about 45 minutes away from one another and neither of us had a car. We would hitchhike back and forth to be together, and when we weren't together, we were connected by phone.

We didn't really know how to be in a relationship, but we were into each other and we tried our best. The road was rocky, and the emotions were high. We were not the best versions of ourselves and with our love sometimes came hurt and pain.

Let's fast forward to the part where we started living inside and got up on our feet – and by on our feet, I mean living paycheck to paycheck, robbing Peter to pay Paul. We were paying our bills but usually carrying balances over from one month to the next. Looking back, we probably could have bought a small house for what we paid in late fees and bounced check fees.

The bowling alley snack bar thing didn't turn out so well. I mean, I could make a great hamburger or a grilled cheese sandwich, but it turned out that making more than one thing at a time was not my forte. I gave it about a month, and one day,

I just didn't go back. I did, however, land a job as a cashier at a 24-hour gas station, one that just months prior had doubled as our washroom. No matter how many hours I could get my name on that schedule, it just never seemed like enough come payday.

It was then that I applied for a loan through the local beauty school to become a cosmetologist. I needed a way to earn more than minimum wage. I liked connecting with women and I was good at hair and nails, so this seemed like a no-brainer. Somehow, and I'm not sure how, I got approved for the loan and began going to school. I worked at the gas station at night and on the weekends and Jerry Patterson worked his ass off doing construction. We had some hope for the future but were absolutely exhausted. Needless to say, the loan went into default and my credit got ruined, but I got that license and soon after, a job in a salon!

More evidence to add to my "I Don't Suck List!"

From Baby Blues to Business Partner

A few years later, Jerry and I solidified our partnership by exchanging vows on the peak of a hill at Brengle Terrace Park in Vista, California, with our loved ones by our sides. Three years later, we gave birth to our first daughter and I thought I had died and gone to Heaven. Me, this dirtbag little girl, who had dropped out of high school and had no worth or value was now someone's wife, the mother of a precious daughter, and someone with the beginning of a career.

Early motherhood, as you probably know, isn't easy, and once Jerry went back to work, I found myself home with a two-week old baby and struggling with the postpartum baby blues. I don't know if I had ever felt so lonely in my whole life. It was then that something strange and truly magical happened.

Check this out!

I was standing in the tiny kitchen of the cottage we now called home. It was 9:30 a.m. and Jerry had been gone for about two hours. The baby was asleep, the house was clean. I had done a load of laundry, hung it out to dry, and was cooking dinner. Did I mention it was only 9:30 a.m.?!

In the other room, the TV was on, and I heard a woman's voice say, *"If you live in the San Diego area and you would like to be a contestant on* Supermarket Sweep, *call us at . . . "* I remember thinking . . . hmmm . . . she seems nice. And then . . . I called her. I was so desperate to talk to another woman that I called the lady from *Supermarket Sweep.* Well, she was lovely, just as I suspected, and while I am sure she was reading from a script when she interviewed me as a future contestant, I was making a new friend. When she asked me to tell her about myself, I told her I had recently had a baby. I'm cringing as I tell you this, but I actually told the lady my entire birth story. I remember thinking, I bet I can keep her on the phone until Jerry gets home from work. I was that lonely.

That was the strange part. Here comes the magical part.

I actually became a contestant on *Supermarket Sweep*! My friend and I won $5,800, and my share of the winnings soon became my first business investment!

It was around this time that Jerry and I were feeling homesick for New York. I was on the phone with a family member there, who was about 10 years older than I was, and was far more financially secure. Her kids were getting older and she wanted to own a business. I remember telling her that she should open a hair salon and that we would move back to New York and I'd work for her! I was so excited about the idea, and then she said, "Let's be business partners."

Business partners? Oh no – you see, I am too young for that. I am not responsible enough. I don't know how to do that. I actually thought I wasn't allowed to own a business. Not sure where I got that idea, but it was deeply rooted in me. It took a little coaxing on her part along with the reality check that while I didn't know anything about business, she didn't know anything about the beauty industry. That made us somewhat equal, so we moved back to New York and I entered into a partnership. I was officially an entrepreneur!

The business did well enough, but after about a year or two, I sold my half to her and moved on. My clients and I adored each other and many of them came to the makeshift salon in our apartment for services. Somehow, doing this completely on my own, in our apartment, felt more like I owned a business than being under the leadership of my former business partner. I was stocking inventory, paying invoices for products, gaining referrals, and charging my worth!

Roles and Responsibilities of the Matriarch

The Matriarch that was coming alive within me began to influence all the corners of my life. I began to see things with an introspect that brought my mind to a place where the effect of each decision lived before I even implemented it.

Let me give you an example. I would ask complicated questions of my then three-year-old with the intention of igniting the insight that I knew existed within her. I wanted her to think deeply and authentically. I wanted her to have opinions, and I wanted to validate those opinions. She was smart and intuitive and the way her mind worked reminded me of Jerry Patterson's. I didn't want her to be told what to think, but rather inspired to think for herself. I wanted to create a message for her that her opinion mattered and that she was worthy of being heard.

When she was four years old, I gave birth to her baby sister, and those two little ladies became my daily focus. The Patterson family was complete! And as much as I loved being their mother, it was no easy task to handle the day-to-day responsibilities and pressures associated with caring for two other humans.

I guess it was good that we were pretty accustomed to things not being easy. We lived in a small apartment and money was super tight. Jerry worked long days doing construction and I started working at night as a doula, supporting couples through pregnancy and birth and caring for mothers and their new babies. A doula is someone who brings physical comfort, education, and emotional support to women and their partners before, during, and shortly after birth. In other words, doulas instill strength and reduce fear for people becoming parents, and I was great at it. Before I knew it, I owned business number two, a doula agency.

Long before I became the CEO of a million-dollar start-up, I became the Matriarch of my family.

Interestingly enough, it turns out that the roles are quite similar. The CEO is the Vision Caster, Fearless Leader, PR Director, and Success Manager. These are the roles the Matriarch plays when the business is called a family.

VISION CASTER

The Vision Caster guides a group toward a future goal. It defines the family's (or business's) brand. If you are someone's mother, you are a Vision Caster whether you realize it or not. You are leading others toward the future and your words and behaviors are powerful.

Shaping the Brand As the Vision Caster, through the development of your "brand," the voice of the family (or business) comes alive. Associations with the brand are positive or negative based on the brand's behaviors. Chapter 6 explains this in full detail but consider a brand like Oprah Winfrey's. Oprah's brand message includes life lessons that remind us that we are enough. That we are responsible for our own lives. Oprah taught us that the soul and spirit matter. That every individual has inherent beauty and value. That where you start doesn't have to be where you finish. Oprah rises each time she falls, and she isn't afraid to talk about it. She's the real deal when it comes to transparency and authenticity, and yet she knows how to keep her private life private.

Take a company like Zappos. Zappos delivers amazing customer service. They are adventurous, creative, and open-minded. They embrace and drive change. They pursue growth and inspire learning. They create a fun and exciting environment for employees, all while remaining passionate, determined, and humble.

We understand these brands because they speak to who we are and what we believe in. Families are no different. A family's brand is what they become known for. It's what they look like, who they collaborate with, what activities they participate in, what they stand for and believe in.

Defining Values   The Vision Caster defines values. In a family that means "In this family, we ..." It's setting a standard. It's building bylaws and expectations. It's creating a vision and helping everyone in the family buy into it. These values manifest through the family's traditions, religion, community service, personal interactions, and behaviors.

Let me share an example with you. When my girls were about 17 and 21, we went to Ty's cheerleading competition. Erica and I were sitting in the stands in the crowded gymnasium with the other parents. Shortly after Ty's team performed, one of her teammates came into the stands to talk to her mom, who was sitting next to us. The mother was proud of her daughter, and when she approached, the mother said, "You guys did great!"

The girl said, "I need money." The woman opened her purse, visibly disappointed by the disdain in her daughter's voice and the shitty attitude that accompanied it. She handed her 20 bucks and the girl turned and walked away. It was awkward. No, fuck that. It was downright disgusting. It was mean, and that woman sat in the sting of it.

She looked at my daughter Erica and shook her head, "Girls ... you talk to your mom like that, too?" Erica quickly responded, "Do I talk to *my* mother like that?!?! Are kidding me? This woman shared her body with me! No, I don't talk to her like that. I would never speak to her like that." The woman found a distraction and let it go.

My children respect me, and I respect them. I remember when they were much younger, and I learned that some kids say "I hate you" to their mothers. I knew early on that if the children I sacrificed for, that I shared my body with, that I wanted more than anything in the world, said "I hate you" to me, it would devastate me. I knew that we needed to be crystal clear that "in this family, we never tell the mommy we hate her," and I worked backward from there.

I sat them down and we had a long talk. I told them about a girl who told her mommy she hated her. I told them how terrible that was for the mommy who loved her daughter so much. I told them how that mommy shared her body with that little girl and how she grew her inside her womb. I told them about this broken-hearted woman who spent every day loving, worrying, and caring for that girl and how she became so sad after hearing the girl say those terrible words. I ended this conversation with the following statement, "In this family, we don't do that." I was clear, I meant it, and as you can see from Erica's response, they received the message well.

Stating the Mission The Vision Caster defines the mission. My family's mission is to build self-esteem and self-worth. We enable empowerment in order to start and maintain sustainable paths while also maintaining a level of loyalty and commitment to the members of the family.

Creating the Culture The Vision Caster defines the culture. This is where we make and implement decisions regarding the way of life and general customs or beliefs by which we function. While excellent does not mean perfect, "good enough," is clearly its enemy. This Matriarch decided early on that good enough just wouldn't do.

Now friends, hear me out on this because this is super important and it will impact you later, I swear. This is where a Matriarch sets clear expectations. Here's one that I set. I made it crystal clear early on to my children that while I walk this earth, I expect them to spend every major holiday with me. It matters to me and I did not want to find myself later without my babies on a holiday because I simply never said it mattered. It fucking matters. I will lay down and die for them without question, I will step up and support them in any and every scenario, I will be there for them with my last breath and my last dollar, and you can bet your ass they're gonna eat turkey with me on Thanksgiving.

Here's another example. My daughters will take care of one another, no matter what. A Matriarch makes sure of that. In this family we don't abandon one another, we work it out; we fix it and we move on. Far too often I see families, siblings in particular, who are estranged from one another. When you ask these people, what did your mother do to help you try and repair the relationship, the answer always seems to be that she didn't want to get involved.

She needed to get involved! Human beings need support and direction, especially as they are evolving into adults. Relationships are hard and we can't quit on them because they challenge or frustrate us. I'm not saying it's easy by any means, but girl, don't quit on your kids' relationships with their siblings. They need you! And they need each other!!

Here's one more. We don't live in a shithole. We all know that kids can get lazy about how they keep their rooms. Unmade beds, clothes on the floor, a cup with some sort of decaying substance in it ... Well not at this Matriarch's house.

The people who live in *this* house are building strong self-esteem and the Matriarch knows that if they settle for living in filth, it will impact them negatively. Yes, I freaked out on my kids. Yes, I'm human, and there was probably a more civilized way to say it, but in this case, the words that came were, "You are far too fucking worthy to live in a shithole! Now get this room clean because you deserve more than this."

It would have been easier to just say, "My house, my rules. I want it clean." But it wasn't about me. I knew what I deserved, and I kept my space worthy of who I was. It was about teaching them their worth and holding them accountable to it.

The Vision Caster is realistically optimistic. In this family, we recognize that hard work and an investment of time, practice, and patience lead us to a positive end result. The Matriarch has the ability to set realistic time frames and recognize the strengths and weaknesses of the team while always working to empower and pull the best out of each member.

THE FEARLESS LEADER

The Fearless Leader sets the course by knowing what she wants for her family's future and leading by example. Fearless Leaders know that they can have whatever they want in this world, if they are willing to do the work to achieve it, and they pass that message on to their children. They also know that it's never too late to switch gears. They explore options and try different things – sometimes for a reason, and sometimes for a season. They are not quitters. They are people who have changed their minds, closed one door and opened another.

When their children ask to sign up for soccer, they teach them about commitment. They say, you may play soccer for your whole life, or you may play for one season. Either way, if we register you, you will commit to being part of the team until the season ends. The team will count on you and you will count on the team. When the season ends, we can reevaluate how you feel.

The Matriarch sets an expectation for others and she delivers on it. I remember being a young mother and working long hours as a birth and postpartum doula. There was a celebration at school, and I was in charge of making cupcakes. Well, like most busy Matriarchs, I figured I'd bake them the night before, after the kids went to bed. I bought all of the ingredients the day before (which, by the way, were a cake mix and can of frosting) and set them on the counter.

But as a doula, I should have known better. I was called to a client in labor in the afternoon and headed to the hospital. When I got home at 1:00 a.m. and walked into the kitchen to grab a snack, I flipped on the light and saw the cupcake shit! This Matriarch had said she would bake cupcakes and as easy as it would have been to say, "Sorry, I got called to a birth and wasn't able to bake," that would have felt crappy to my daughter and to me.

So, I baked cupcakes, cleaned up, went to bed, and four hours later woke up, frosted them, decorated them, and delivered them. The most important thing you should know about this life event is that it went right on my "I Don't Suck List!" It contributed to my strong self-esteem and my relationship with my child. Those are the things in life that matter. Well … cupcakes matter too!

The Fearless Leader Solves Problems You don't have to have your shit together to do this. If you're a mom, you do this every day. You realize you're going to be late getting the kids off the bus. You call a neighbor and ask if she can grab your little persons when she gets hers. She is happy to oblige, and you ask for her Starbucks order so you can thank her properly. You solved the problem! Give yourself a round of applause, problem solver!

Some people solve problems by getting someone else to do it. Others solve problems themselves. Case in point, you realize you are $600 short for a major car repair. You recognize that you could call a loved one and borrow the money, but you also recognize that you are capable of figuring it out yourself. So you do the following: You think, *How can I make some extra money?* You take a walk through your house and consider what items you can sell. You reach out on social media to see if anyone has an odd job you can help out with. House cleaning, childcare, running some errands, etc. You are resourceful, and you use those skills to solve problems. Give yourself a round of applause, problem solver!

The Fearless Leader delegates tasks and empowers the team. Everything for a Matriarch is about enabling empowerment in others. When my 12-year-old needed a doctor's appointment, I had her call to schedule one. She was the patient and customer. She had a voice. She had value. And she had the respect of the person receiving the call. A Matriarch wouldn't have it any other way.

THE PR DIRECTOR

The PR Director has a sterling standard of discretion. This really matters. I remember as a kid, my mom would talk to the women in her life about everything. Some of those women were her friends and some were my aunts. I'm glad she had women in her life that she felt comfortable with during that time because I understand the importance of a support network. But she hurt me. Deeply.

Every time I got in trouble, every time I made a mistake, every time I acted on a bad decision, she told these women. I wanted these women to love me, to see me. I wanted my own relationships with some of them, and my mother kept putting my worst foot forward to them.

A Matriarch shows her loyalty to her family first. She recognizes that her people deserve privacy as they navigate difficult times in their lives. She protects them from the judgments of others, and she fosters their growth. She doesn't gossip about them and she doesn't let others do it either.

The PR Director develops and maintains strategies that are intended to uphold the "clients" image. In this case, the client is the family. It begins with NOT doing the following: One day, while waiting for an appointment, I was sitting in the reception area and there was a woman reading a magazine. Her son, about three years old, was playing with a toy that was comprised of thick colored wire and wooden beads. He was sliding the colorful beads and watching them land on the other stacked beads. He had the sweetest grin and a curiosity that was so charming. I looked at the woman and said, "He's so cute!" She smirked back, and right in front of the boy, she said, "You want him? He's yours!" Now I can only guess that she was joking, but I was stunned by the words she chose, and I'm sure he was too.

Imagine you're all dressed up at a cocktail party with your husband. You're standing by his side in your most gorgeous dress, crammed into a pair of Spanx beneath it. You're sporting a phenomenal up-do and professionally applied makeup. He introduces you to his co-worker and the guy says, "Wow, your wife is gorgeous." You shyly smile and your husband says, "You want her? She's yours!"

Yeah, I thought that might help you see this differently …

If the family is your "client" and you are the PR Director, what message about the client are you conveying when you offer to give one of its members to a stranger?

The PR Director controls and coordinates the events of the family. Scheduling the social calendars of each member, party planning, carpool arranging, volunteering, meal planning, and so much more all land in the lap of the Matriarch. She not only steps up to the plate, but she knocks it out of the park. Somehow, even under stress or with the flu, from the car or from the throne (otherwise known as the toilet), this chick gets it all done.

The PR Director builds a network. If I had a dollar for every new struggling businesswoman who told me she wasn't good at networking, I'd be sitting on a private jet right now traveling to some exotic location while eating cupcakes and getting a foot massage.

Here's the thing, you've been building a network your whole adult life! A Matriarch builds a database of professionals, personal acquaintances, and friends who evolve into the social calendar for the family, as well as opportunities for jobs and community service. We used to keep a Rolodex (look it up), alphabetically filled with every person we knew.

Now we have Facebook; a simple, "Who do you know that fixes cars and won't rip me off?" and you've got choices and solutions galore.

Can't network, my ass …

SUCCESS MANAGER

The Success Manager praises success and redirects or corrects unsuccessful behaviors and mind-sets. Now, I never said this stuff was easy, but it's gotta be done, and the Matriarch has to do it. We have our faults and so do the people we love.

When it comes to our children, we must guide them with authority. They are sorting things out for themselves and need our help. They are figuring out big lessons like cause and effect, actions and consequences, right from wrong, and they are developing a personal culture within the family culture. Because culture is a crucial part of our identity and it is largely shaped by those we surround ourselves with, we must acknowledge that our children are influenced by others and have many identities. The Matriarch, however, is the greatest influencer in her children's lives and, as such, maintains an open mind and a forgiving heart.

She may joke that she rules with an iron fist, but what she means is that when she is asked a question and she responds with a "no," it never means maybe, and it is never overturned.

One day when Ty was about seven years old, she had a friend over after school. They were playing inside, and I could tell by the laughter and energy in their voices that they were having a great time. As it approached the hour that the friend's mom was coming to pick her up, the two happy girls appeared in my kitchen. I was just starting to make dinner, when what I could tell was a well-thought-out, thoroughly premeditated question was about to be asked of me. "Mom, can she stay for dinner?" "Oh sweetie, not tonight but we can plan it for a day next week." Ty said, "OK, mom."

Suddenly the other little girl began doing this really strange thing. She bent her arms and clasped her fingers near her chin. With a big grin on her face and this odd jumping motion, she began bouncing all over my kitchen reciting the word, "please" over and over again. Ty looked at her nonchalantly and said, "We don't do that here. She doesn't change her mind once she says no."

At seven years old it is pretty easy to navigate this stuff. You make the rules and the people follow them, right? Well, I mean, if you insist on them and you don't waiver from them. You got that part, right? But as our children grow, the choices they make and the behaviors that accompany them are more difficult to navigate. A Matriarch is invested in their future and she works to be sure that they know she has their backs. She is a soft place to land and she knows what to do next. She enforces a consequence that involves a lesson and she knows that positive self-esteem is always the goal. She doesn't embarrass them, and she doesn't destroy them socially, but they get the message loud and clear.

■ ■ ■

Now I'm not perfect, and like any exceptional CEO, I made mistakes, but like Oprah, I rose each time I fell. The more in tune I became with my inner Matriarch, the more I accepted the role, and the more I readied myself for one day stepping into my title as CEO of a multi-million dollar start up.

Now, please don't misunderstand me. Being the Matriarch of your home and family does not negate your partner's role in any way, nor does it mean that I wore the pants in the family. In my house, if I was the CEO, then Jerry Patterson was the President of the Board of Directors, and in many ways I answered to him—not because I was subservient, but because my husband is a strong and brilliant man. He is level headed, research based, totally grounded, and usually right. And that is sexy as fuck to me.

It's about checks and balances and maintaining stability. The President of the Board of Directors keeps the CEO in check, and while I am certain that that has been no easy task, to say the least, that is exactly what he has done. He is my supporter and encourager. He believes in me. When fear creeps in, he assures me it will be OK. When I feel defeated, he points out the lessons I've learned. When I point out my flaws, he points out my strengths. My gratitude for this man knows no end. We have done life as a team and his influence has helped shape me into the Matriarch that I have become.

Matriarch Must-Do #4

Take an inventory of the roles of the CEO and find examples in your own life of how this title is one that you've been wearing daily.

Chapter 2

A Matriarch's Future Is Based on Her Actions Today

We are all defined by our previous actions and what my history indicated was that I was a quitter with low self-worth, who put herself in vulnerable situations and didn't care about the future. That is what I showed people and that is what people believed about me.

Now imagine where I'd be if I hadn't made the decision to create some new history. Let's face it, the very next time I stuck out my thumb on the side of the road could have easily been my last day on earth.

It's interesting how things always begin with a decision, right? And now it's time to make some more. Let's decide together, right now, that we are living a day that will become part of our history. Let's live it like we will tell the story of it tomorrow to someone we admire. And let's make damn sure that we get to tell them a story we're proud of.

If I could transform my shitty history of a dirty kid on welfare, who smoked weed, listened to heavy metal, dropped out of high school, and didn't achieve much of anything, into a story about a down-and-out-but-deceptively-smart chick who gets her shit together, marries her soul mate, raises confident daughters with amazing self-esteem, creates a clean and loving home, and runs a successful business, without sacrificing my love for tattoos, hot pink stilettos, and Metallica, then you can surely create some new history that better defines you, too.

Let's write some Matriarch-level shit by living some Matriarch-level lives!

There are five concepts that I want you to make your own:

- ◆ Take history-changing actions.
- ◆ Tally your successes.
- ◆ Write the story of you.
- ◆ Live each day to the fullest.
- ◆ Protect your dreams with your life.

Take History-changing Actions

Let me give you an example of how I made a decision that changed my history. First, let me tell you that I will remember this pivotal life moment until the day that I die. I couldn't forget it if I tried, because this single history-changing incident made me feel more like a fucking rock star than almost any other life event I have ever experienced.

It was a cold and rainy day and I was in the thick of parenting two small children. The girls were about six months and four years old and we had just made our weekly grocery store trip. The cart was filled to capacity with Ty in the wagon's front seat and more bags than it was designed to hold in the back. Erica was holding on to the back pocket of my jeans as instructed so I wouldn't lose her, and I was navigating what felt like a 200-pound cart through a cold, windy, and rainy pothole-filled parking lot.

I got to the car and put the girls in their car seats before unloading the groceries. One by one, I took each bag out and set it in the car. Whew! Almost done. Just one more bag. As I lifted that last bag and twisted to put it on top of the paper towels, I saw it ... a corkscrew strapped to a piece of cardboard that I put in the wagon during the early part of my shopping trip.

Immediately, I realized that this item, this stupid corkscrew, this $9 twisted piece of metal, never made it onto the conveyor belt. My first instinct ... so what? No one knows. Just throw it in the car and get the hell out of here. My next thought was, *Maybe it's a Mistake.* So I got into the car, pulled out my 14-foot-long receipt and frantically scanned it in search of the words, "1 Corkscrew."

As I'm sure you can guess, it was to no avail. No corkscrew on the list, no $9 payment. And that's when it happened. I took an action that day that not only rewrote my history but became part of the story that I am fiercely proud to share with you today.

I got out of the car. With the wind blowing in my face so forcefully that I struggled to breathe, I opened the back driver's-side door and whipped that six-month-old girl onto my right hip. We ignored the rain pounding down on us and walked around the car to the passenger side, where I opened the door and had my four-year-old hop up onto my left hip. I asked her to hold the corkscrew and proudly said, "Mommy made a mistake. We accidently left the store without paying for this and we have to go back in and give them the money." This from a girl who previously left stores with items not on the receipt as a hobby, just because she could get away with it ...

I had become a woman with principles. It didn't happen that day, but it revealed itself that day through my actions. I hadn't had an epiphany where I said, "I now have principles." I wasn't even thinking about it. Instead, I was changing and growing and as my self-esteem and self-worth were developing, I was becoming a woman with integrity. And now I had proof!

I had new history that indicated strong moral character and that filled me with pride.

A history-changing action is packed with power. When you start taking these kinds of actions personally and professionally, you'll start leading the life you always wanted to.

I told myself for a long time that I wasn't good at paperwork, or details, or the computer, and I let my fear of learning about new technology hold me back. I once got fired from a job for it, which created some hardcore evidence that I wasn't capable of learning new things. But at some point, I wanted to grow, so I had to start learning. I had to take new uncomfortable actions in order to create the future that I desired.

I had to abandon my fear that pressing the wrong key on a computer's keyboard would cause me to blow up the world. I learned how to send e-mails. (BTW, I know how ridiculous that sounds ...) I learned how to read a contract. I learned about search engine optimization and long-tail keywords. And low and behold, those actions that I started taking manifested into a successful future.

When I stopped mentally listing all of the things that I wasn't good at, I made room for more things that I was good at. I stopped procrastinating on going to the DMV because I was no longer afraid of not knowing how to choose and fill out the right form. And before I knew it, I stopped getting tickets for having an expired registration sticker on my car.

Fear is paralyzing and we procrastinate on the things we are afraid of or that we find difficult. The things we believe we are good at always get done first. If you rewrite your history by taking new actions today, you can reclaim your confidence and the list of things you're good at will begin to grow. Imagine the level of productivity you'll achieve when you face your fears and start taking history-changing actions.

Tally Your Successes and Not Your Failures

Imagine that you spent an entire summer researching a new business idea. Let's just say it was beekeeping. You were excited to learn about smokers and veils and the supreme power of the Queen bee. You filled notebooks with ideas about the natural beauty products you would make: Lip balm! Hand cream! Soap! The possibilities were endless. You could see yourself at the local greenmarket in a flowery vintage dress, selling your locally sourced honey in mason jars adorned with labels lovingly designed by you.

But it turns out that that beekeeping suit you'd need in order to avoid getting stung to death was more pricey than you thought. And wow, keeping a hive alive is a lot more work that you anticipated ... Before you could say "Etsy shop," your conversations with your girlfriends morphed from beeswax candles to what's happening on the latest episode of *Scandal*. Your passion for beekeeping died before it ever produced a drop of honey.

Building a business is hard-core and it takes a lot of self-reflection. It takes a tremendous investment of time, energy, and usually money before it ever comes to fruition. Just because you decide one particular line of business isn't for you, it doesn't mean you can't be an entrepreneur. Who cares if the chapter of your life titled "Beekeeping" ended before it even got started? It's no big deal. You learned a ton of shit about bees and that's cool. So, good for you.

Not every idea is going to be a million-dollar idea. A wise entrepreneur flushes out the weak or flawed ones before making the financial investment. Yeah, I'm calling you a wise entrepreneur.

A true Matriarch doesn't tally her failures; she celebrates her successes. The beekeeping business decision to not move forward IS a success! You didn't go in the hole, you didn't kill the hive, and you didn't get stung by a bee! Eat a cupcake, bitch; it's all good.

ACKNOWLEDGE A SETBACK AND MOVE ON

Being the Matriarch of a busy family and building or running a business is no joke, but it's beautiful work. And because of the amount of "stuff" you hold in your head at any given moment, sometimes something slips through a crack. Something that as a Matriarch you deem important.

Let's say you planned to take a package of chicken out of the freezer before leaving the house in the morning, but you got distracted by a phone call from a potential client. Phone in hand, potential client engaged, you grab your bag and head out the door. You hop in the car, open your planner, and schedule an appointment.

You hang up the phone and you drive off. Later, on a call with your husband, he casually says, what are we doing for dinner? And you realize there is a frozen block of chicken cutlets in your freezer that never made it out. You shift gears. You don't crucify yourself. And you certainly don't say, "Ugh I'm so stupid." Instead you say, "Hey! I'll grab the kids after basketball

practice, and we'll meet you at China Gourmet! Sound good?"
You're human. You're busy and you are a fucking Matriarch.
Your family will be together, you'll have a great meal, and all
will be well in the world.

We have got to start shifting our focus from tallying our
failures to tallying our successes. You may have fucked up in the
past, but think about all the shit you've done right. A Matriarch
is a ship that can't be sunk ... and by a ship, I mean a $5 billion
yacht.

No Failures. Only Lessons, Growth, and Wins

Tallying our successes is a place where earlier in life we got
a bad message that we saved to our hard drives as Dont_be_
conceited.pdf.

Tallying our successes was "conceited." When I was growing up, the worst thing someone could say about you was, "Oh
my gosh, she's so conceited." So we worked hard at not celebrating our achievements. We deliberately did not acknowledge
our accomplishments, but somehow ALWAYS acknowledged
our failures. In fact, when someone acknowledged our accomplishments, we usually pointed out our failure in it.

Here's an example.

You: Lisa, I love how you help your children see the lesson
          in every scenario.

Lisa: I know. I just wish I didn't get so frustrated with them
          in the process.

LISA! Knock it off! Accept the compliment! You're a kick-ass
mom just like you hoped you'd be! Own it! This chick sees all
of your hard work. Kudos to you, Lisa. Stop downplaying it and
teach your friend how to do what you do so well.

Let's pause and take a moment to recognize that every single
thing you ever do, every decision you ever make, is something
you can learn from, grow from, or succeed at. A Matriarch takes
risks and is constantly evolving. This means she'll never experience failure, only lessons, growth, and wins. Say it with me ...
No failures. Only lessons, growth, and wins.

Write the Story of You: A Woman Destined for Great Success

Because I understand that what I do today directly impacts my life and my business tomorrow, and because I want a good ROI (return on investment) on each 24-hour period that I live, I give each day my all. I'm happy to go the distance by spending time on the phone with a potential client who I know won't hire me. I know that she'll speak well of me and someone else will hire me because she did it. Leaving it ALL on the table when I teach a business class to a room full of entrepreneurs results in more attendees at my next class. When I do a couple of loads of wash during the week, I don't become overwhelmed by Mt. Laundry on the weekend.

When I think about ROI and where I can invest for the best return, it is always in myself. Whether I am investing in my education or in my self-care, I know it will pay off. You see, everything I do today becomes part of tomorrow's story, and the story has the potential to get better and better every day.

Crafting a story that casts you in the spotlight as a woman destined for great success is not a show for others. Instead, it is about staying motivated and feeling alive enough each day to go out and do it again. If I wake up and think, *Fuck, it's morning. This house is a wreck. I forgot to buy coffee. The dog peed in the hallway. The kids forgot their lunch*, and then my Facebook memory reminds me that last year at this time my life sucked too, then I'm not likely to make the most of this day.

But if I wake up and think, *I ate well yesterday, and my body feels good! I'm gonna wear those fitted black slacks with my smokin' hot mesh pumps! I get to meet with my favorite client today! I'm having lunch with some really sharp colleagues*, then I'm gonna feel like this day is all mine and I'm gonna make it my bitch!

Being conscious of the story you are crafting is a crucial step for the Matriarch who wants to see herself and her business succeed. Are you a woman who unknowingly and unintentionally inspires people with your attitude and actions, or are you a woman who seemingly has given up on themselves?

Your Social Media Story

Social media is specifically designed for you to craft a story about yourself. What would I know about you if I became your Facebook friend or I followed you on Instagram?

Are you crafting deliberately? Are you telling the story of "I need wine to cope"? Would I see a post from you about how you wished your kids were back in school at summer's end? Are you a woman who shares commentary like "He left me"? Would I see you as a complainer? A whiner? Does fatigue and exhaustion define you?

Or are you crafting a story that highlights the positive? Would I see your gratitude? Would I see your esteem and your worth?

"Ahh ... Crisp night air and fresh sheets on my bed make for the best night's sleep!"

"A long talk with a good friend and everything feels right in the world!"

"Treated myself to Starbucks and treated the cashier to my bubbly personality!"

This is possible even during the most difficult of times.

"Had a rough day but tomorrow looks promising!"

"When my son whispers the words 'You're the best mommy' in my ear after a looooong drawn-out temper tantrum, my heart simply melts."

"Sadness makes me so grateful for happiness."

Think about the product or service you're selling. Are you representing yourself as an expert in that field – on those topics? If you do childcare, are you posting pro tips about caring for children or are you posting frustrations about your own? If you're a wedding photographer, are you posting about the magnificent bride you worked with last week or do you bitch about bridezillas?

Or are you an interior designer who makes YouTube videos in your home and is 100% cognizant of how well-curated the design elements are in each shot? Are you a hairdresser whose own hair is always sugar sharp, healthy, and on trend?

People want to network with and pay for services from people who convey accountability and self-respect. If you're not personally conscientious and accountable, the message you're conveying to the consumer is that you are unreliable.

So Matriarchs, let's kick it up a notch. We know that no one wants anyone in their life who constantly bitches and complains, right? It's draining. Those people literally suck the life out of you. They're like giant life buckets with holes in the bottom of them. Every ounce of energy they gather seeps out the bottom. If I just described you, repair your fucking bucket! No one wants to engage with or do business with broken, ungrateful, energy, sucking people.

Success Is the Reward to Those Who Are Authentic

I believe that you are a woman destined for great success. I also believe that as you shed the skin of the beliefs and opinions of others and you find your own voice, you will truly begin to thrive. It's time to stop allowing others to lead you like a dog on a leash. You are a grown woman with your own values, beliefs, and ideas, and it's time to start living in your own truth.

I mean c'mon, peer pressure is dead. It died back in high school. So why are you holding on so tightly to it? Why do you care what *they* say or think? Who the fuck are *they* anyway?

We succumbed to the influence of others in school because we were desperate to fit in. That no longer is the case. What matters now is what *you* think. What *you* believe. What *you* desire. You owe no one a reason or an apology. You are the boss of you. You decide what is and isn't acceptable. And you stop judging how you feel on the inside against how people seem on the outside.

An authentic life is one lived in comfortable skin. Now slather on some moisturizer and let's get to living!

Live Each Day to the Fullest, and Feel Like You Absolutely Slayed It

Look, a day moves quickly, and if you're not careful, you can end up feeling like shit at the end of one. So you have to be super cognizant about living each day to the fullest. Girl, you've got to get back to living this life of yours and being grateful for the opportunity to do so. Day after day is slipping through the cracks and you've got nothing to show for it but a checklist with the same shit on it for the past three months. Today is YOUR day and you're gonna live it to the fullest!

So grip the throttle with your right hand and pull it all the way back! Feel the wind in your hair and the vibration under your ass as you start living life with the volume on 10! No more holding back, OK?

This means waking up with a plan to seize the day. It's consciously deciding who, what, and where is most deserving of your time. It means not wasting your entire day on the "social scroll."

You need to dig deep into the soil of your relationships, with yourself first and those you love second. You have to discover and develop your purpose in life and do something every day that validates who you are and why you're here. You have to stop avoiding the things that intimidate you and uncover why you feel intimidated. You have to set goals and take steps every day that get you closer to reaching them.

You have to connect deeper and laugh longer, meet new people, and do good deeds. You have to put yourself out there and get a little vulnerable. You have to stop settling and start stretching.

You see, we all have good days and bad days, and if we're deliberate about what we do with each one, we'll start having more good than bad. Try living in the moment for a minute. Sit in a bad moment and say these words to yourself, *I have the power to change this*. And then change it.

Crank up the music and belt out Bon Jovi's "Livin' on a Prayer" and tell me you still feel shitty … It's just not possible.

Write something, draw something, create something, love something, share something! Just do SOMETHING!

Ask yourself, *What does living this day to the fullest mean to me?* Know what it looks like for you and be prepared to work toward it.

For me, it means looking, feeling, and behaving like my best self. It's pouring into others and working feverishly to reach my goals. It's morning coffee with my husband and check-in phone calls with my girls. It's a great lipstick and a pair of stilettos. It's rockin' out to Metallica and connecting with the Matriarchs in my life. It's lifting someone up and helping someone out. Its smiling without covering my mouth and not apologizing for who I am. It's not comparing myself to others but instead holding myself in high regard. It's working toward a higher level of consciousness and a deeper spiritual connection. And it's about copping some gratitude at the end of it all because each day we get to do these things is a true gift and we're gonna start treasuring it. Got it?!

Protect Your Dreams with Your Life!

A Matriarch doesn't tell her friends and family about every new idea she has (like that beekeeping one), but instead nurtures her ideas and brings the best ones to fruition. It's part of how she creates new history.

But it takes an enormous amount of self-esteem that most women don't fully have (yet), to pursue something when the people who love you say you shouldn't. How about that time you decided you were going to become a doula? You excitedly told your friends, only to hear them say, "What's a doula? I never even heard of that. Is that like a midwife? I can't imagine you doing that ..."

You were so confused by the combination of your interest and enthusiasm and your friends' negativity that it resulted in your making no decision at all. You didn't decide to take the doula training AND you didn't decide not to. You simply let that dream die. You had the ability to bring it to fruition and instead, the voices of your friends held a pillow over its head and choked the fucking life out of it. Becoming a doula went from the front of your mind, to the back of your mind, to completely out of your mind. You were robbed and it was your friends who robbed you.

Their lack of desire to see you change resulted in you letting go of something that mattered to you. People fear change. It's that simple. If you change, how will it impact them? The people in our lives are strong influencers, and when we have an idea or a dream, we must also know that we need to protect it. You cannot let the people in your life determine the trajectory of your future. If they are risk averse, they will always work to prevent you from taking a risk. Real support comes without bias or judgment, and unless you're positive that the person you're going to share with is going to provide that level of support, don't share it.

And while we're talking about this, do you do this shit to other people? Are you a dream stealer? If you are, knock it off!

A truly supportive friend will offer a positive brainstorming, mind-mapping interaction that encourages you to see all possibilities and challenges while working to help you find solutions that support your desires. Anything less than that is negative, and you know the saying: no risk, no reward. So bitch, get off my reward!

You must practice self-control. Keep your mouth shut until you've made a definitive decision. If you're an external processor, and you are the kind of person who can't spend a day with your people and not share, you may need a business consultant. This person is objective and doesn't have any bias regarding what your life looks like with this idea in it or out of it. The business consultant's role is to strategize, plan, and problem solve, helping you to determine what your next steps are.

A Matriarch never takes advice from anyone who isn't where she wants to be.

Chapter 3

The Four Big Lies

Now that I've presented you with some evidence of how capable you are and I've taught you about the power associated with making a decision, do you think you can stop lying? The lying is just out of control. All day long … lying to yourself and every other person in your life. I know this sounds harsh, but so is all of that lying. It's time to start saying what you actually mean, knock off the self-deception, and stop lying to your friends and family.

Can you stop saying, "I'll try" when you mean, *I won't?*

Can you stop saying, "I'm too busy" when you mean, *I won't make time to?*

Can you stop saying, "I can't" when you mean, *I don't want to?*

And for the love of all things pizza, can you stop saying "I had no choice" when you know damn well you did?

Look girl, I know you. I know who you are, and I know where you've been. I've been there too, and I said the same shit. But if we're gonna be friends, and I feel like we are at this point, then I've got to call you out on this. Whether the people in your life buy into your deceitful ways or not, they're clearly padding your corners and cushioning your falls. They are allowing you to live in these lies and accepting them as your truths. But where's that getting you?

I'll tell you. You disappoint others, which in turn, disappoints you, and it chips away at your self-esteem and self-worth, which you've already learned are essential to becoming a Matriarch. You cut off your opportunities and limit your choices, which is destructive to your future success. You create additional, but false, stress for yourself, which eats you alive physically, mentally, and spiritually. And you limit your growth, which contributes to the idea that you are a failure.

But hang on, let me prove something to you.

Women lie to me all the time by saying they can't sell. I know it's a lie. They say things like, "I don't like sales. I'm not good at it. I just don't want to seem pushy." But check this out.

Ya know how you get when you're really excited about something? You'll be having lunch with a friend and she'll ask what you did over the weekend. That's the only cue you need to start telling her about the mind-blowing meal you had at the new restaurant that just opened. You go into full detail about everything from the perfectly crafted cocktail and the sexy lighting, to the chocolate dessert that was so good, you slapped your husband's fork away when he reached for a bite.

Women know how to sell shit to each other, their partners, and their children, and they do it all day long. Remember the time you and a friend got the idea that you should go on a double date with your husbands. You knew damn well your husband would rather have his eye plucked out with a fork than sit through an awkward dinner with this new friend applicant you were suggesting. But you carefully crafted your sales pitch. "You guys have so much in common! He likes football too! He works on old cars! You guys will get along great! I really like her, and I want us to be couple friends!" You're quite a saleswoman, ya know.

To this Matriarch, it just sounds like a big fat excuse when you sit in your shit and blame your imaginary inabilities for where you ended up. You've created an opportunity to be pissed off because life just happened to you and you were the victim of it. Poor you …

You'll try …

You're too busy …

You can't ...

You had no choice ...

Ugh ... It sounds so gross. So fucking pathetic. Shake it off! Girl, you are not the victim here of anyone but your own way of thinking. And today, you start anew. Today, you grab that bitch by the throat and you tell her, THIS FAR AND NO MORE! Today you take back the power invested in your ovaries and you take charge of your thinking. Today, you tell yourself the truth and let the lies fall to the wayside. You're back, and I for one am ready to celebrate with you!

Buckle up, girl, cause I'm about to show you how to replace the four big lies with some new and improved empowering truths! You ready?? Let's go!

Lie #1: I'll Try

"I'll try" is a procrastination technique. It's a stall tactic and it serves no one, not even you. It sets you up to disappoint the people in your life and it gets their hopes up that they will spend time with you or that you'll come through with a favor. You know you won't when you say it, but you take the seemingly easy way out.

There's nothing easy about letting people down, and when you do, it adds to the evidence that you are incapable. If you're serious about this Matriarch thing (and you should be) then you are focused on building evidence for your "I Don't Suck List." Every time one of these "I'll try" lies slips out, and you don't accomplish what you said you would try to, you create more evidence that you are not capable.

Did you ever *try* to take a shower? Did you ever *try* to walk the dog? Did you ever *try* to eat a sandwich? No. You didn't. You took a shower. You walked the dog. And you ate a sandwich.

But it's even deeper than that! There are actually three levels of "I'll try" lies, so let's explore them now.

The Blatant "I'll Try" Lie.

I know I'm not going to your stupid Tupperware party because the minute I walk in the door after work, I take off my bra and whip my hair into a bun and there's no chance in Hell I'm putting that titty torturer back on to go to your house and ooh and ahh over burping plastic containers.

The Soft "I'll Try" Lie.

I think I can, but I don't want to fully commit right now. This is the "I'll try" lie you use when someone asks you if you can do them a favor. Let's say you and a friend are having coffee. You say you've got to go, that you've got some errands to run. She asks where you're going. You tell her you're stopping at the pharmacy and then running to the liquor store to grab some wine. She says, "Oh! When you're at the liquor store, if the owner is there, you know, the guy with the long beard, can you ask him if he'll donate a wine basket to the fundraiser?" You feel OK about it and you think to yourself, *Yeah, I know him well enough to ask, but sometimes it's weird there* and you just don't want to commit. So you pull out the soft "I'll try" lie in case it feels awkward.

The Escape Clause "I'll Try" Lie.

It's used when you really want to (*right now*) but know that you could change your mind and you don't want anyone holding you accountable to your word. Here's how it plays out. It's Saturday morning and you see your friend in the grocery store. She has enough hamburgers and hot dogs in her cart to feed the entire neighborhood. You suddenly remember that tonight is her annual summer bar-b-que, where she does in fact feed the whole neighborhood, and she says, "Will we see you tonight?" Quickly you whip out an escape clause "I'll try" lie that sounds like this, "We're so excited! We're really gonna *try* to come." She smiles and says, "Do your best, we'd love to have you." And you confirm the escape clause "I'll try" lie with, "You throw the best parties! We'll do our best to *try* and make it."

Now imagine what it would look like if you said, "No, I hate Tupperware parties." Or, "OK, but if the guy is weird, I'm not asking him." Or, "I'm not sure if I'm up for a party, I'll text you if I'm coming."

Somehow, you've been conditioned to believe that lying is less mean than telling the truth. That, my friend, is also a lie! It's become second nature to tell these lies. You must dial in to your first nature, which was to be authentic. You know, honest. Remember that?

On a professional level, "I'll try," is your business's kryptonite. As an entrepreneur, I am my own point of accountability. If I say, "I'll try," I'm saying it to myself, *I'm the boss and I know what I am capable of when I actually do try.* So if I say, "I'll try," and I don't deliver, I know damn well I didn't try.

I've been teaching business classes to entrepreneurs across the country for years and I've seen women disserve themselves by not being honest over and over again. They say, "I'll try to get my website built by the end of the month," but "I'll try" doesn't represent a strong commitment to getting anything done.

Get honest about what "busting your ass" really looks like. If it means working two days a week, your business will likely experience part-time success. If that's your goal, perfect. But stop lying to yourself and then not meeting your own expectations.

The last thing I'll say about "I'll try" is that it has absolutely nothing to do with being too busy. If your daughter's wedding is this weekend, don't tell your business partner that you'll *try* to follow up with a lead. Be honest. Tell her that you're consumed with last minute details for the wedding and you won't have the time to invest in an intake call that a new client deserves.

When you feel compelled to whip out an "I'll try" lie, stop and ask yourself these three questions:

- ◆ Why am I lying?
- ◆ What variables will prevent me from accomplishing it?
- ◆ Why won't I commit?

Lie #2: I'm Too Busy

I'm busy. I am a loyal and committed wife and mother. I'm the co-founder and CEO of a seven-figure start-up. I host an annual conference. I travel regularly for business and pleasure.

I write with deadlines. I maintain my home. And yet, somehow, I'm able to consistently manage my social media accounts and watch my favorite TV shows. The point is, I've been busy when something important came up, and you have, too. And we figured out how to add it to the roster.

Let me tell you about something that was really important to me. When my children started school, I started a tradition. A tradition that would become part of our family's culture and one that I believe will be passed down from generation to generation.

Each year on the very first day of school, just before each one of my girls got home, I took a tray of freshly made chocolate chip cookies out of the oven. I would sit at the table with them as they dunked those warm cookies into an icy cold glass of milk and licked the melted chocolate from their fingers. They would share the details of their first day with me and it gave me great insight into who my little ladies were becoming. It was important. I did it every single first day of school from kindergarten to 12th grade. I made a commitment.

But here's the thing. I was busy. No, like, really busy. I was attending births and supporting new families as a doula; I was managing a team of other doulas and running a business; I was the Girl Scout leader for both girls' troops; I was on the Building Steering Committee at their school; I was the cheerleading coach, etc., etc.

There were years where I raced home to mix the cookie dough and slam it into the oven with seconds to spare. There were years where I could have said, "I was too busy," and they probably would have understood ... But it would have been a lie.

How often do women hurt themselves or others with lies like this? I'm confident that not only can you relate, but I'm also pretty sure you'd be able to provide some personal examples, if asked.

How We Hurt Ourselves

What we are actually doing when we whip out an "I'm too busy" lie is lowering our standards. We're accepting the idea that we are unable to adapt, manage our time, and organize our schedules, and that leads to lower esteem. If you are not too busy, don't say you are. Say something else. Like the truth! Say you aren't going to make time for it. Say it's not important to you. Say you just don't want to. But stop saying you're too busy.

It's as simple as this. You don't want to stop eating junk food, so you don't make time to plan your meals. You don't want to exercise, so you don't make time to go to the gym. The idea of these things may sound great to you, but lying to yourself by saying you're too busy to do them is bullshit, and you know better.

How We Hurt Others

We hurt others with the "I'm too busy" lie because they see right through it. They know you're really saying you don't want to and that feels personal. When we say, "I'm too busy" to someone asking for our company, our support, or a favor, they hear us say, "I won't invest in you," and that hurts them. Why not just say the truth? "I can't lift heavy furniture." "I don't want to see that movie, but I'd love to go have a drink instead." "I can't talk right now, but I can call you back in an hour." That wasn't so bad, was it? And no one got hurt.

This "I'm too busy" lie is complicated and there are two parts to how we use it.

Part 1—The Front End of the Lie

The front end of the "I'm too busy" lie gets you out of doing something before you commit to it. Check out the five categories of the front-end part of this lie:

The "It's Not Important to You" Category   This is when you recognize that what you're being asked to do is important to the other person, but not to you. They want you to go look at paint swatches with them for their new kitchen, but the idea of standing at the paint store while they choose between 17 shades of off-white makes you wish the earth would open up and swallow you whole instead. Her kitchen's paint color is just not important to you and you're not gonna make time for it. But girl, make no mistake about it, "I'm too busy" is a flat out lie and she knows it.

The "Too Invasive" Category   This is when you just don't have the head space to imagine yourself doing all that it will take. Let's say your friend just became a Thirty-One Gifts consultant. You mention that you really like the products, and she starts telling you about the hostess gifts you could receive by hosting a party for her. Immediately your mind starts racing. That means displacing your family for the evening, cleaning your house, inviting everyone you know to come, buying cheese, crackers, fruits, and veggies, and then prepping them all, *AHHHHH!!! No freakin' way!* Instead of saying, "That's more work than I'm willing to do," you lie ... "I'm too busy ...," but she knows the truth. Unfortunately, she interprets it as you just aren't supportive of her new business venture.

The "I Don't Want to Do It" Category   That's it. You just don't want to, and that's OK. On a different day you might want to, but today, it's a no. Instead of just saying, "Girl, I'm just not into it today, I hope you understand," you worm in some bullshit about being too busy. Knock it off! She understands. There are times when she doesn't want to either, and she gets it. Stop with the lies!

The "I Don't Like the People" Category   This one holds a tremendous amount of power. You don't want to go because there will be people there that you don't know, like, or want to meet. You like a tight circle. You don't want to go to the thing where the people are that you don't know. You might have to talk to them ... Gulp ... You might make a new friend. You might build your network. It might be good for you. But, no, "You don't like the people," so you play the "I'm too busy" card. The truth is, you know your friend would try to talk you into coming if you told her how you felt and you don't want to take the risk, ya liar.

The "I Won't Enjoy It" Category You think it's important; you're just not gonna enjoy it. Like the time your dad said, "Aunt Julie would love it if you called her once a week, just to say hi. It would mean so much to her." You love Aunt Julie, but you cringe at the idea of a forced small talk session, so you hit him with an "I'm too busy" lie and hope he lets it go. It sounds like this: Gosh, Dad, I would love to, but I just barely have time for this call with you. I'm just too busy. ← Liar, liar, pants on fire!

PART 2—THE BACK END OF THE LIE
The back end of the "I'm too busy" lie is used to get you off the hook when you don't come through with something you agreed to.

Check this out …

You're working with a therapist; her name is Karen. She advises you to read a particular book that she believes will help you navigate your fear of success. It's important to you, so you write the title in the notes section of your phone so as to not forget. After all, you're paying Karen to help you eliminate this fear, you trust her, and you're excited about digging into this book.

The following week, you arrive at your appointment and she asks you about the book. You heat up. You realize it fell off of your radar the minute you walked out of her office last week. And now, you're embarrassed. You disappointed yourself and you feel like you failed in some way and you don't want her to know, so you hit her with a back-end "I was too busy" lie. You say, "Ugh! Karen, I was too busy to stop and get it. I'll get the book this week."

You leave, get in your car, and call Barnes and Noble. They don't have the book, but they say they will get it for you. They call you two days later and say the book has arrived.

The next week, you show up for your appointment and Karen asks again about the book. You panic. In your mind you scream, *Fuck! The book!* You look your therapist in the eye and with that, back-end lie number 2 flies out of your mouth. "Karen, I ordered the book from Barnes and Noble, they got it for me, but I've been TOO BUSY to go pick it up."

Week three, you're sitting in the reception area of Karen's office and she opens the door to welcome you. As soon as you see her face, the thought explodes in your head, *THE BOOK!* It's right in your bag. You've been carrying it around since you left here last week and went to pick it up.

The problem is, wait for it, you've been TOO BUSY to read it. Oh girl, you a mess.

Here's the deal. You wouldn't keep finding yourself in these situations if you stopped back-end lying and just owned it.

Because a Matriarch knows that her failures don't define her, she handles it like this:

"Karen, I totally blew it. I'm so glad you're my therapist. This is one of my biggest issues. I just can't seem to prioritize the things that will benefit me most. Do you think we can focus on this over the next couple of weeks? It's really a problem for me."

And guess what? As a result, the Matriarch grows!

When you feel compelled to whip out an "I'm too busy" lie, stop and ask yourself these three questions:

- ◆ Is "I'm too busy" the truth?
- ◆ What are you trying to avoid?
- ◆ Are you lying to save face?

Lie #3: I Can't

Who the fuck told you, you can't? And why on earth did you believe them? Now, I'm not talking about saying "I can't" when someone asks you for a favor and you tell them you can't do it with a personal reason attached to it. What I'm talking about is the defeated whiny, *I can-n-n't* that you tell yourself. The one that you speak into your mind, body, and spirit and allow to rot your capacity for living.

In your personal life, it's: *I can't say no to my kids ... I can't control my appetite ... I can't stay on top of the laundry ... I can't remember appointments ... I can't save money.*

In your professional life, it's: *I can't write good blogs ... I can't speak in front of people ... I can't learn to use new technology ... I can't talk on the phone ... I can't ask to be paid more.*

Stop lying! You simply choose not to! It's time to take your power back. You don't want to do something? Don't do it! But stop saying you can't. It's literally tearing apart the self-esteem that you're working so hard to build and maintain.

MEET THE TWINS—I DON'T KNOW HOW AND I GIVE UP

You know you're guilty of it; we've all been at one time or another. You approach a task or a challenge with a whiny "I don't know how ..." and if by chance you actually step up to try to figure it out, it's not long before you land a bitter "I give up."

I Don't Know How For many reasons, we regularly block our own success by convincing ourselves that we don't know how to do things that other people do. Whether it's because we're afraid that we'll fail or that we'll succeed, fear seems to be the thing that holds us back more often than anything else. So let's imagine we have no fear, that fear is no longer able to hold us back. Calm down ... You can have your fear back in a minute. What would be the first thing you'd tackle?

In the meantime, let's look at some of the other reasons we say, "We can't."

It's too hard!

OK, it's hard, I get that. Maybe it's physically hard and you need a friend to help you. That doesn't mean you can't; it just means you can't, *alone*. Don't put off what needs to be done by saying you can't. Make recruiting a friend to help you a priority and tell yourself you did it, instead!

Maybe it's hard in the sense that it's complicated and there's research that you must do in order to figure it out. You are resourceful now, remember?! You recently heard of this new thing called the World Wide Web and it turns out they have tons of information there! In fact, they even have this website where you can learn damn near anything by watching a video! It's crazy, I know …

Stop saying "You can't" because you're afraid that it's too hard.

You're not inspired.

In this day and age, if you're not inspired, it's because you choose not to be. You can't look at any form of media and not see an inspiring story, meme, or message. So the problem is not that you're not inspired. Inspiration is every-where – open your eyes. But it takes a shitload of it to ignite motivation. Motivation is personal and no one has the power to engage it but you. Feed your soul with inspiration and open your mind to receiving the motivation you need. That's what it will take to eliminate the lack of action that comes with the "I can't" lie you've been telling yourself.

You don't want to—but didn't give yourself permission to say so.

Psst. We don't do the things we don't want to do. You know that, right? So why not say you don't want to diet instead of saying "I can't lose weight." Why not say you don't want to create a budget and stick to it, instead of saying, "I can't save money."

All this "I can't-ing" is draining your power, and, and, girl, you need that fucking power! These "I can't" lies just require some resourcefulness on your part. They need to be figured out and you, my friend, are capable of doing it. You simply can't con-vince me otherwise, and as soon as you stop convincing your-self that you can't, doors will begin to open for you that you never imagined walking through.

I Give Up   Oh baby, nothing is more devastating to a Matriarch than watching another woman give up. You see, we know each other's potential. We know what each other is capable of and yet, when it comes to ourselves, we just can't see it. Watch me break down this list of lies.

I can't keep going.

No? You can't keep going? Did you ever watch *The Biggest Loser*? You know, the show where morbidly obese people, out of sheer desperation, submit themselves to the diet and training programs developed by exercise gurus Jillian Michaels and Bob Harper? These people beg, cry, and puke as they insist they *can't*. It's simply a tactic used by a person who desperately wants to give up on themselves. They can. It's a lie. And the trainers prove it to them.

I can't do one more thing.

Yes you can. You absolutely can wash one more dish, make one more meal, write one more e-mail, make one more phone call, or whatever else is necessary. Stop quitting on yourself with this lie. This defeatist attitude looks gross on you so shake it off, wouldja?

I have no self-control.

This is the lie you tell yourself when there is one more donut in the box and you regretfully eat it. You had control and you ignored it. Ignoring something or not using it doesn't mean you don't have it. Think about all of that exercise equipment you have. Just because you ignore it and never use it, doesn't mean it's not in the closet. Just sayin'.

I can't meet the need.

Your child has an issue and it's really complicated. From doctor to doctor and therapist to therapist you just can't seem to get an answer. His behavior and symptoms continue, and you just want him better and your life to feel normal. It's overwhelming and it's kicking your ass. I get that. You need support. Probably more support than you even know. But you are working to meet the need. You are doing All. The. Things. Stop lying to yourself by saying you can't meet the need. You are, girl, and we see you.

I can't explain.

This is just a cop out. You can explain how you feel, what your position is, what your needs are.

You may not have someone who wants to understand them, but that doesn't mean you're not capable of doing it. It just means they're an asshole! Stop bearing their burden by lying about your ability to communicate and find someone who wants to understand you instead!

Overcoming "I Can't"

When things are hard or you just want to give up, you must do something different. You hire a coach. You partner with people who don't give up. You build an inner sanctum of people who don't let you off the hook, even when you want to let yourself off the hook. You dig deep and you create reminders for yourself for those times when you want to throw in the towel.

You do a self-care check in. You ask yourself, *Which self am I most concerned about right now?* The "tired, I need to rest" self? Or the "I will succeed" self? Of course you should meet the need of the self that is speaking the loudest. But under no circumstance should you delay a goal or not reach a deadline because you simply needed a mental health moment, hour, or day. Take the moment, hour, or day – just don't let it turn into weeks, months, or years. Time moves quickly whether you use it to your advantage or you simply rest it away.

Let's stop saying, "I can't," and reserve the words "I'm not able to" for circumstances where we are truly not able to do something.

For example, we are not able to be in two places at one time. If we are previously committed, we must say we are unable to accept an invitation. If we are ill, we are not able to care for someone else's children.

When you feel compelled to whip out an "I can't" lie, stop and ask yourself these three questions:

◆ Can I figure it out?
◆ Am I giving up?
◆ Am I genuinely unable to do it?

Lie #4: I Had No Choice

For this lie, I don't have too much to say. The bottom line is ... this is bullshit, so knock it off. You always have a choice. The problem is, you may not like any of the choices. But to say you don't have any takes away all your power; it's limiting and stifling. So, stop it, OK?

Nearly every woman in America has a choice. When I was living outside, I wasn't equipped with a skill set so my work options were cooking hamburgers or pumping gas. Admittedly, these were pretty limited options, but they were options nonetheless.

The point here is, the language we use impacts our esteem. Stop saying, "I didn't have a choice," and start saying, "I made a decision." This lie is simply a strategy you use to convince yourself that you are not responsible for the decision you made. Maybe it wasn't the right one. Maybe it was the wrong one, but it was better than not making one at all.

The only time you don't have a choice is when you don't use your power to choose – when you choose *not* to choose. And even then, that's a choice. If you are alive and not in a coma or do not have severe brain damage or an illness that has left you completely disabled, you ALWAYS have a choice. If you're able to read this book, you have a choice.

When you feel compelled to use the "I had no choice" lie, stop and ask yourself these three questions:

◆ Did I use my power to choose?
◆ Was there an alternative decision I could have made?
◆ Do I recognize how this lie disables my power?

■ ■ ■

Women use these four big lies to cover up what I call "chump feelings." Chump feelings are those messy emotions that knock you on your ass and dump you into a negative mental place. They're personal to every Matriarch and can include, but are by not limited to, envy, jealousy, and awkwardness. They make us think, *Why me?* Or, *Why her? I suck. She sucks. This is impossible. I'm not good enough. I'm not worthy, I'm not capable, I don't have power*, and so on and so forth. None of them are true and you're not a chump. You have feelings. Acknowledge them. But stop allowing them to hold you back!

Matriarch Must-Do #5

1. Become mindful of the language you use.
2. Set a mental alarm for each of the four lies that is triggered by your use of them.
3. Capture the lie the second you release it and ask yourself, *What's the truth?*
4. Work to get the alarm to sound just before the lie leaves your lips.
5. Refer to yourself as a truth-telling Matriarch.

Chapter 4

A Matriarch Owns Her Decisions

S o picture this. I'm at the mall, and I walk into my favorite
store, Free People. Note the name: "Free People." Like, PEO-
PLE who are FREE, right?

OK, here we go. I take my first lap around the perimeter
of the store and get a feel for the space. That's kind of how
I shop: It's my second lap where things start to click. So I'm
coming around the back of the store on my second trip and I
see something that catches my eye. I stop and check it out. It's
a gorgeous double-breasted teal blue velvet jacket with silv …
Wait! That's not the point here.

What I'm trying to tell you about is that within earshot, I
could hear the following conversation taking place between two
women. One had tried on a handspun knit V-neck poncho. It
was short sleeved with long fringe encircling the bottom. It was
made of an earthy blue with two thin white bands and a grey
stripe between them. At the neckline were two long blue strands
made of the same handspun yarn that tied together as a low
"necklace." I was totally diggin' it. The woman was standing in
front of a mirror checking herself out from every angle while
her friend watched.

Woman in poncho: I love this poncho! Do you think I'm a
woman who wears a poncho? I mean …

	Would I actually wear it?? Oh, I love it! What shoes go with it??? Hmmm, I dunno … it's on sale …
Friend:	Do you think you'll wear it? What do you have that goes with it? I mean, it's not really you …
Woman in poncho:	I don't know … I just love it!
Friend:	I mean if you really like it …?
Woman in poncho:	What would you think if you saw me wearing it? Would you think I was a weirdo?
Friend:	I would think you like ponchos …
Woman in poncho:	Yeah, I don't know … Maybe I'm just not that girl.
Friend:	I don't think anyone is that girl …
Woman in poncho:	Yeah, you're right; it's stupid.

Now imagine me, Randy Patterson, a modern-day Matriarch, standing there watching this. I'm in total disbelief. This woman is having a self-identification moment and is desperate for someone to co-sign her desire for more authentic self-expression.

You see, this woman has spent her whole life trying to fit into the box of other people's expectations for her, but deep inside, there is a beautiful, long-haired, spirited woman, dancing in the rain in a poncho trying to break free. And all she wants is someone to validate her – a co-signer who will tell her it is safe to come out.

I'll be honest with you; it hurts my heart just to share this story with you because I know unequivocally that this woman does not need a co-signer. What she needs is confidence and self-trust.

So many women want someone to validate their choices, to affirm that they are making the right ones. A Matriarch doesn't need anyone to co-sign her decisions. She knows that opportunities open for her when she's in tune with her life and her business practices. A Matriarch makes decisions. Now that doesn't mean she's always right, and sometimes she changes her mind – but the decisions are hers and that's empowering. A Matriarch is able to make branding decisions, she can hire an architect or a graphic designer, she can choose a paint color, and she can buy a fucking poncho! And she can do it all without having anyone co-sign it for her.

This is especially important for women entrepreneurs. Starting a new business or taking one to the next level can be scary as hell – and it can stretch even the most valiant of Matriarchs. There are investments to be made, people to hire, vendors to pay, legal matters to manage, and so on.

There will definitely be moments where she stops and wonders: Am I making the right decision? And that's good. Sometimes there is "cause for pause" and we must stop and assess. For this, we must seek out wise counsel.

Wise counsel never co-signs. Wise counsel is the person in your life that you know or hire who has an expertise in the area where you need to make a decision. They assist you in finding *your* right answer. Wise counsel can often see things because of their experience and expertise that the average person cannot see.

When you're in a rut, a co-signer will help you choose curtains and furniture to decorate the rut, but what you really need is wise counsel. Wise counsel helps you strategize ways to climb out of the rut.

Meet Suzie, a Woman in Need of Wise Counsel

Suzie is in the life rut of having three children under six years old. Her days are long and exhausting and filled with words like, "No-no. That's not nice. Mommy said no. Put that down. I said no. Leave that alone."

Suzie's house never feels clean, she never seems to get to the bottom of that pile of laundry, and the dishwasher is broken for the third time this month. Steve, Suzie's husband, gets home and somehow, she manages to slap a meal on the table. The evening ensues and three tantrums and one broken light saber later, everyone is asleep. Finally ... Suzie is exhausted. She gets undressed, gets into bed, and Steve wants to fuck!

Like any red-blooded American overworked, under-appreciated, stay-at-home mom with three kids, trying to supplement the household income with her direct market sales business, she says no. Steve feels rejected. Gets pissed off. Goes to sleep on the couch. And Suzie feels abandoned.

The next day, Suzie calls her friend Kristen. She chooses Kristen because she knows Kristen gets it. She lives it, too. Her kids are two, three, and five, she's a stay-at-home mom who goes to nursing school at night, and she's equally as exhausted as Suzie is. Suzie gives her the play-by-play and Kristen feels her pain. She listens as Suzie rants about how her days suck the life out of her and how Steve does nothing to fill her cup but expects her to fill his ... Suzie is pissed, and Kristen agrees that she should be. In fact, Kristen feeds Suzie's fire. She says things like, "He's such a dick. Doesn't he see what a great wife you are? You even make money. My husband would be so happy if I was bringing money into the house. Why doesn't he appreciate you?"

And just like that, Suzie has been co-signed.

Her instinct was to be angry with Steve, and Kristen not only agreed, she encouraged it. Suzie feels validated, affirmed. But, that's NOT what Suzie needed! That may be what she wanted, but it certainly wasn't what she needed.

What Suzie needed was wise counsel.

Now if you have ever been where Suzie is, and I'm gonna guess you have, this is what wise counsel would have looked like:

It would have come in the form of a woman who is a minimum of 10 years Suzie's senior. A woman who not so long ago had been where Suzie is and made it to the other side. Let's call her "Jenni." Jenni would look Suzie deep in the eyes and say, "Breathe Suzie ... Good, now talk to me. Tell me something you love about your life."

Jenni would remind Suzie that she has some things to be grateful for. Suzie would tell her she loves being a mom but it's really hard. Jenni would acknowledge that and tell Suzie that she is not expected to love every phase or every moment of her life. That there are challenges and that strength comes from enduring these challenges. Suzie would tell Jenni that her husband has expectations, but by the end of the day, she is exhausted from giving to others.

Jenni, as her wise counsel, would suggest that Suzie pause, that she shift gears. That she consider her husband's touch and affection an opportunity to receive something, rather than to give something. Jenni would help to open Suzie's eyes and encourage her to dig deeper. She would remind Suzie that there is a bigger picture here. She would enable Suzie to realize that when she looks back on these times, it will be the big picture that she sees, and not these individual frustrated moments. Jenni knows this firsthand because she lived through it and made it to the other side. Her sheer existence gives Suzie hope and breathes new life into her, and Suzie continues on.

Wise counsel is a person you turn to who has a level of expertise or personal experience in a specific area of life where you are struggling and need the wisdom they can provide. These people can come in the form of acquaintances, friends, family members, mentors, business coaches, and occasionally even strangers.

Imagine this. You've been inspired by HGTV after years of watching *Flip or Flop* and *Fixer Upper* and have been saving to invest in your very first flip. Your real estate agent is working hard to help you find a great opportunity. She finally comes through with something affordable that has seemingly great potential. You go see it and you feel super excited. There are a couple of red flags but since you have no experience, you're not sure if they're valid. You really want the house. You thank your realtor and say you'll get back to her.

Next, you call your co-signer, and we're not talking about someone who co-signs a loan. We're talking about the person you think you can get to talk you into this purchase. You call her and sure as shit ... she delivers.

You've been co-signed. You feel validated. But girl, that's not what you need.

What you need is wise counsel. Here's what wise counsel looks like for this particular scenario:

It comes in the form of an experienced trustworthy contractor, an appraiser and/or a person experienced in flipping houses. They share their wisdom with you, and you ask your questions. They remind you to make a decision that is based on facts and figures and encourage you to remove any emotion from this purchase. Buying this house is not about making you happy, it's about making you money, and your wise counsel knows that, even with your enthusiasm leading the conversation.

The Co-signer: Does She Co-sign Your Agenda or Her Own?

A co-signer is someone you call to say, "Talk me into it." or "Talk me out of it." Someone who just wants you to feel affirmed and validated. They actually think they're doing you a favor. When you're tired, they talk you into staying in bed. When you say you're overwhelmed, they encourage you to take something off your plate; when you want to quit, they tell you it's OK.

They tell you to practice "self-care" and imply that that's what you need, but it's actually not. It's a cop-out. I for one don't want people in my life that validate my bullshit. Sure, tell me to give myself a break for a day or two, but also tell me to shake it off in the morning and step back into my powerful self!

Often, we seek a co-signer as our emotional support person. They know us well, they love us, and they want the best for us … as long as it's what *they think* is best for us. But we must consider that they are not able to be objective about the support they offer. They're too invested in us and they have their own desired outcome.

Think about that time your friend told you about the 468th fight she had with her boyfriend. She wanted you to co-sign her in-the-moment feelings. She was pissed and she wanted you to hear her. So, she came to you for emotional support.

You felt her anger and it inspired yours. You said, "How many times are you going to let this happen before you walk? This guy is no good for you. You have to leave. He's a total asshole." You co-signed her in-the-moment feelings, but also saw it as an opportunity to push *your* will on her in a weak moment. She doesn't want to leave this guy; she just wants you to co-sign these feelings she's having. Emotional support should come without bias and should be objective.

Wise Counsel: She Paints the Big Picture without an Agenda

Wise counsel is someone who makes you think. Someone who enables your empowerment by helping you see the big picture. Someone who asks you questions that lead you to *your* right answer. They don't tell you what to do, but rather help you see things more clearly. Somehow, after speaking with them, you feel wiser – more confident, more prepared.

This person has no agenda. They don't really care what you do one way or another. Take their advice, don't take their advice, they are wise enough to know that your decision will only impact you and not them. They are completely objective and that's what you need.

You don't need anyone making decisions for you. You are a Matriarch, and, girl, you've got this!

Confidence Is Key

Since everything about your personal and professional success revolves around confidence, now is probably a good time to talk about how positive self-talk will enable you to get some or grow some more.

I'll be honest with you: There have been times where I have found myself on the verge of a decision and my confidence wavered. Times where I hesitated, where I questioned myself and my abilities, and my "self-talk" took over. Fortunately for me, my self-talk usually sounds a little like, *Fuck it. Just do it!*

But if that's not the language or form that your self-talk takes on, you're going to need to preload a canned response for these situations. Maybe yours sounds more like, *This is safe, and you'll be fine.* Or, like, *You've got this. Go for it!* Whatever it is, it must be in your own voice.

You are the most credible person you have. Regardless of what your inner voice says, you will believe it. So make damn sure you dial your self-talk station in to the Modern Matriarch Channel.

To Thine Own Self Be True

It begins with this statement, "To thine own self be true," and we have William Shakespeare to thank for it. When we are true to our core values and beliefs, we gain and remain confident. When we waiver on these important inner systems, we lose confidence.

Here's an example:

Cherish just took a newborn photography course. She's super excited about offering this new service! She put time and a considerable financial investment into the course. She paid for childcare, drove to and from, paid for parking, bought meals and paid very close attention. The course was brilliant, and she left with great insight. She felt confident and equipped.

She purchased props for her shoots, a new lens, additional lighting, and changed her marketing materials to include newborn photography. She checked with her insurance agent and business attorney to see if she needed to make any legal adjustments, and she set up her price list. Now, she is ready to start marketing!

Cherish joined some Facebook groups specific to newborn photographers. She wanted to see how others were marketing their services and join the conversation! Another member posed this question:

"What packages do you offer and what are your prices? Please also share how long you've been doing this!"

Excited that she had organized her prices, Cherish replied. She shared her packages and price points and the fact that she had just taken the training to offer this type of photography, but she hadn't actually acquired a client yet.

Well, that's all it took. Within minutes there was a waterfall of comments all directed at Cherish:

"Those prices are more than what a seasoned expert charges ..."

"How dare you price your services at similar rates to professionals ..."

"Wow ... full of yourself, much?"

They just kept coming and Cherish felt shittier by the minute. She began to question her beliefs. Her core value of charging her worth was being challenged, and you know what Cherish did?

She quit that Facebook group, sought out wise counsel, and moved the fuck on.

But imagine if Cherish had lacked confidence. Imagine if strangers on the internet had the power to destroy Cherish's self-esteem and redirect her entire business model. Unfortunately, we see it every day. Women let go of their personal beliefs because the voices of others are louder. Let's use Cherish as our example to stay true to ourselves and never waiver simply because other people see things differently. It's just Facebook, you guys. Never let a social media platform rob you of your authenticity. Protect that shit with your life! There is a "block" feature for a reason. Use it!

Do You Look Confident?

I know it sounds lame, but you've got to fake it till you make it, and looking confident is not about impressing others – it's about convincing yourself. How can you possibly believe you're an awesome esthetician when you don't take care of your own skin? How can you believe a client with a half-million-dollar budget will choose you as their Realtor when you look like you live in a shack and there are sunflower seed shells all over the floor of your car? Get your shit together, OK? You can do this.

FACE A FEAR AND CONQUER IT!

C'mon now, start small and let's see what you've got. Choose a fear and beat the ever lovin' shit of it! Maybe it's learning new technology. That's a big one for lots of us. Decide what you're going to learn, get on YouTube, search it, and learn it. Each time you learn something new, challenge yourself to pick something else and do it again. Dig deep and explore every avenue until you find yourself becoming more and more confident. Before you know it, you'll have a larger skill set and more abilities. Don't wait on this! You could be smarter by the end of the day!

BE PREPARED!

When you walk into a meeting with 16 colleagues and you're the only person who says, "Does anyone have an extra pen? I forgot mine," you instantly feel like a fourth grader whose report card says: "Is often unprepared for class." This is no way to start a meeting where you are expected to boldly share ideas. Get yourself together beforehand. Don't wait until 30 seconds before the meeting to grab a coffee and run in the door. Read over your notes, gather your thoughts, and get a fucking pen!

WHEN INSECURITY RISES UP, RECOGNIZE IT AS THE BULLY IT IS

Look, we're not gonna get through this life without glimmers and sprinkles of insecurity. We're human and I think it's normal to occasionally feel a bit insecure. But don't let insecurity bully you out of the game of life and place you on the bench. You're in the game, girl. You are a starting player in this game! In fact, without you, the team has to forfeit. If insecurity makes you a bench warmer instead of a starting player, you will miss every opportunity to score the winning point and we can't let that happen, right? Acknowledge insecurity when it rises up into your chest. Recognize it. And then, move on.

AFFIRM YOURSELF WITH POSITIVE SELF-TALK

If you tell yourself you're a loser, you will lose every time. You must, and I repeat, you must talk to yourself like you like yourself. Maybe that's difficult right now, but imagine that the you that you're speaking to is your 13-year-old self. Imagine that her esteem is low, and you want to build it up. Only speak to your-self with words you would speak to her with, and before you know it, those will be the only ones that come to mind:

> *Self, you are wise and strong, and you are growing more fierce every day. Love, Yourself*
>
> *Self, you are enough. You are worthy and loveable, and you are an asset to everyone who knows you. Love, Yourself*
>
> *Self, you are our priority. When you love you, we will grow and thrive. Put you first! Love, Yourself*

SET A SMALL ACHIEVABLE WEEKLY GOAL AND ATTAIN IT

No excuses, no lies. This can be as simple as handing out three business cards a day or committing to writing a weekly blog. Choose something that you have a tendency to slack on and grab it by the balls. When you are deliberate about getting something done, and you do it, you feel accomplished. Once you prove you can do it, add it to your "I Don't Suck List" and it will contribute to a higher level of confidence for you.

TRUST SOMEONE WHO BELIEVES IN YOU

There is someone in your life who believes in you. A teacher, a friend, a family member, a mentor. She thinks you've got something special and she is your biggest cheerleader. Trust that this person knows what they're doing! Trust their words about you when your own words aren't enough. It's not from sympathy that people say positive things about us, ya know. It comes from them observing our actions and attitudes. Trust these people. They know what's up!

Decision-making 101

Making decisions builds confidence. And if you take nothing else away from this book, take that. Now let's be clear, I know that different people make decisions different ways and I am smart enough at this point in my life to know that screaming at you to "Just make a decision!" isn't how it's gonna work.

There are four ways that people make decisions and I want
you to think about which one you identify best with.

1. Go with your gut

Some people have a natural tendency toward deci-
siveness. They are dominant in personality style and they
easily trust their instincts. They are not afraid to commit
to a choice. They are deliberate, driven, determined, and
often demanding. These people are intuitive, and yes or
no, up or down, black or white, is not only easy for
them, but comfortable too. They feel productive when
they are making decisions and don't worry about being
wrong. They know that if they are wrong, it can be fixed,
and life will go on. These people can be difficult to get
along with and can cause other decision makers great
amounts of stress.

2. Social acceptance

These people make decisions based on what others
do or have done. They are influential and interactive by
nature and love the inspiration of personal stories from
those they care for and respect. Decision-making is very
involved for this person because the result of the decision, and how it appears, really matters to them. This
person is an out-loud processor and seeks the approval
of others. They want recognition and they enjoy being
the focus of attention, so decision-making becomes a
group effort.

3. Security minded

This person struggles with decision-making. They
have a tendency to avoid it because change is difficult
for them. The fear of the unknown far outweighs the
discomfort of the current situation, so this person often
does not decide. When they do work to tackle decision-
making, they have a propensity to talk themselves into
something and then right back out of it with the next
breath. This can go on for weeks until the opportunity to
decide is ultimately lost. Because they are so concerned
by the impact their decision may have on themselves and

those they love, they fall into the "overthinker" category and often miss out.

4. **Research and evidence**

These folks are cautious. They are extremely contemplative, and they have a process for decision-making that requires full-fledged detective skills. They make decisions based on evidence and credibility. They are careful and calculated and also quite capable. They don't typically focus on the emotions of others in the process but rather on what is the best possible outcome and how do they reach it. The process can be lengthy but that doesn't matter when you are being thorough and concise.

Which one of the four best describes you?

Now that you have a clearer understanding of your behaviors, you can begin to create your own strategic process for decision-making.

If #1 best describes you (Go with your gut), then clearly you are confident enough to make a quick decision. Girl, you don't need a strategy, you simply make a choice. Congrats on being a badass decision maker!

If #2 best describes you (Social acceptance), then you know that having a partner in crime for decision-making will serve you well. You are people-oriented and like to work in a team. Don't wait until you are confronted by a proposed decision and then frantically gather opinions. Know who your person (or sounding board) is and you'll be more efficient in arriving at your conclusions!

If #3 best describes you (Security minded), then your goal is to not miss opportunities because decision-making is too challenging. The tips below for working through decision making will benefit you tremendously.

If #4 best describes you (Research and evidence), then you've got what it takes. The trick for you will be not getting so far down the rabbit hole of research that you lose sight of the decision that needs to be made. There is such a thing as "too much" research, and you'll have to be careful not to let that happen. The tips below can help keep you on track.

WORKING THROUGH A DECISION

As you now know, for some people decision-making is a breeze. But if you are someone who is struggling, the following tips are for you.

1. Ask yourself, *Do I actually have to make a decision at all?* If the answer is yes, know exactly what you need to decide.
2. Use a support BRA (I'll explain in a minute) to gain clarity and understand your options.
3. Consult your end goal and mission.
4. Compare against your values and principles.
5. Seek wise counsel.

Let's use a haircut as an example and use our newfound decision-making tips as a guide! This will be fun!

First, we need clarity. So we ask ourselves, should we get a haircut? For the purpose of this exercise, let's decide that we are in fact getting a haircut and we have decided that Amira at "Waves for Days" is going to be our chosen hairdresser.

Now, let's check our support BRA. BRA is the acronym for Benefits, Risks, and Alternatives, and it applies to every decision we ever have to make. Let's apply it to this haircut.

Benefits—What are the benefits to getting a haircut? Well, our hair will be healthier, more manageable, current, and fresh.

Risks—What if we get a shitty haircut and we hate it. This could make us feel terrible and we would have to wait for it to grow back.

Alternatives—What are the alternatives to getting a haircut? Well, we could just not get one. Or we could color our hair instead. Buy some accessories; a wig maybe.

Next, we need to think about the end game. What do we expect this new hairstyle to do for us? We just landed an amazing new job in a corporate environment and we want to look polished, but we also don't want to lose our femininity. We like our hair long enough to fit in a ponytail when we exercise. (I mean as long as we're using our imagination here, why not imagine that we exercise …) So the mission is feminine and professional with a bit of length intact. End goal and mission? Check!

Next up is to compare against our values and principles. Since we are the kind of woman who just landed a corporate position, we know that we will need to be somewhat conservative about our appearance, and that aligns with our values and principles. Check!

Lastly, we are going to seek wise counsel and, in this case, that's Amira! We got incredible recommendations for her from friends who are her clients. We checked out her website; she looks amazing and professional. Her photo gallery of previous clients is spot on. Amira is our girl! Seek wise counsel? Check!

Decision made! Now all of the work that went into making this decision helped us make it, but it doesn't completely eliminate the chance that Amira will have a bad day and give us a shitty haircut. The work we did will remove much of the risk, but with decision-making always comes a bit of risk – but that's ok because we can handle it, right?

No risk, no reward, and you are on the path to great rewards.

Chapter 5

Attention! We No Longer Work for Free!

S ometimes it happens without you even realizing it ...
You're off to a great start! You woke up at 5 a.m., poured yourself a cup of coffee, and sat down to tackle your e-mails. You answered the woman who had questions about her upcoming photography session. You sent off a contract to a new client. You e-mailed information about packages to a potential client interested in a session. You made all of your kid's lunches and threw in a load of laundry before anyone else even woke up.

This day is yours and you are determined to live it to its fullest!

You got the kids dressed with minimal meltdowns, dressed yourself, whipped on your favorite lipstick, and arrived at school with plenty of time to spare.

You're outside chatting with some of the other moms when the woman we'll call "Sharon" ambushes you.

"Ohhhhh. You're Kimberly? You photographed my neighbor's daughter's first birthday party, and oh my gosh!!! Those photos were amazing! I'm so glad I ran into you; you absolutely must photograph my daughter's Sweet 16 party! Please tell me you're available June 22nd?!"

Your ego lights up from her gushing about your work. You're excited to hear that word is getting out about your new business.

73

You've been a professional photographer for years, but only recently opened your business and started marketing it.

That birthday party was your first event since you opened. Taking photographs is your passion, and the shots you got at that party were amazing. You're thrilled that the client is talking you up to her friends! You quickly check your calendar, tell Sharon you're free that day, and secretly high-five your own badass self!

Sharon is one of the most connected women in town and photographing an event for her will be a monumental score for your business. You hand over your beautiful new business card and tell her you can't wait to jump into the details of the event with her.

Sharon e-mails you later that day, reiterating her excitement, and adds that if this works out, you could do some work for her successful real estate business. You love the idea of a steady gig working for a Realtor like Sharon. You respond enthusiastically, and attach your pdf detailing the packages you offer, your pricing, and your standard contract. You reread your draft for typos and confidently hit SEND.

And that's when it happens ... Sharon drops the, "Oh, I thought this would be free ..." bomb.

Before you respond to her e-mail with a simple "These are my rates," Sharon hits you right in the gut with her admittedly sexy argument that this "arrangement" will benefit both of you. You see, she needs an amazingly talented photographer, and you need to build your reputation and clientele, no? She tells you that your photographing her daughter's Sweet 16 party (for FREE) is an OPPORTUNITY for YOU.

She dangles the glittery golden carrot that is her amazing list of contacts, and before you can say Roger Rabbit, you've sunken your teeth in and taken a giant bite. You burp out a quick "Uhhh yea, of course ... ," and suddenly that carrot you're chewing on tastes like bitterness, resentment, and regret.

What the fuck have you done? You know damn well that you didn't open a business so you could work for free and now you feel like a total asshole.

You've agreed to spend an entire Saturday away from your family, to capture a milestone moment in another family's life, FOR FREE. You're probably going to need an assistant for an event this size and that will be money out of your pocket. This event is now actually costing you money that could be used for guitar lessons ... or gas, or groceries. It will take hours to sift through the images, choose the best shots, and then ... the editing. Hours and hours of FREE editing ...

You try to make yourself feel better by telling yourself that all of this work will result in countless referrals that will lead to paying clients. You work hard to convince yourself that it will all be worth it in the end. That's the lie you'll cling to for dear life as you "bless" Sharon and her daughter with your FREE services ...

We All Want a Bigger, Better Boat and Working for Free Is Not How We'll Get It!

I've heard countless versions of this bullshit scenario as I've traveled the country working with small business owners. The idea of working for free is especially rampant in birth work, and it's one of the reasons I started offering business-training courses for doulas. The truth is that until women collectively understand and demand to be paid what they're worth, we'll all be in the same leaky, crappy boat that's barely staying above water.

I want you in a seaworthy vessel that's as steady and as amazing as you are. Make no mistake here, I'm not judging you. But I know that your time, training, expertise, and presence are worth a whole lot more than you're charging.

Most Matriarchs find themselves at some point or another agreeing to do something they wish they didn't. It happened to me ... Many years ago, when my girls were little and I was a busy mom working overnights as a postpartum doula, a friend asked if I could watch her daughter before school two mornings a week. Her daughter was the same age as my oldest (five at the time).

This friend thought the girls could have an hour and a half of "play time" at my home starting at 6:30 in the morning ...

And then, I could get them on the bus and send them off to school. I justified it by telling myself that this friend "needed" a favor and that the girls would have "fun" playing together.

Well, it was a fucking nightmare. We dreaded the fight-club-style play dates that occurred on Monday and Wednesday mornings and it didn't take me long to realize that we were ALL making a huge sacrifice to accommodate this friend ... for FREE! I quickly realized this "favor" had to end. These mornings sucked the life out of me. That's when I decided that going forward, when this bitch worked, she was gonna get paid!

WORKING FOR FREE BECOMES PART OF YOUR BRAND MESSAGE

The very second you agree to work without the pay I know you deserve, FREE becomes part of your brand. Whatever it is you do – photography, birth work, writing, childcare, graphic design – the moment you agree to attend a birth, design a business card, or rearrange someone's living room to maximize their feng shui without pay, you become known as the woman who does it for free. Let's face it, word gets around – especially when you're giving away free shit that normally costs a shitload of money.

THE WORKS–FOR–FREE STIGMA: DON'T LET IT TAINT YOU

Let's go back to our girl Kimberly for a minute. Let's assume she photographed Sharon's daughter's Sweet 16 party, and because she's amazing, her pictures are stunning. She captured every moment, big and small, and managed to get a family photograph that included all three generations. Absolutely priceless! And literally priceless because as you recall ... Kimberly gave her services away for free.

So, while Sharon got beautiful photographs of a major life event, Kimberly actually missed out on a softball game where her daughter slammed a triple. Surely Kimberly's selfless act should result in a torrent of highly paid referrals from Sharon, right? WRONG. Time and time again, what happens in such circumstances is something more like this:

Let's say Sharon is chatting with a client of hers who is opening an art gallery and needs some promotional photos taken. Sharon says, "I have just the person for you, gallery lady!" To say Sharon was happy with Kimberly's work is an understatement – she could practically write a power ballad about her daughter's Sweet 16 party photos, that's how much she loved them.

"But oh wait, did I mention that in addition to doing fantastic work, Kimberly is just starting out, so she does it for free!?"

Gallery lady is in! A great photographer who is building her portfolio!? What an amazing opportunity! Sharon passes along Kimberly's contact information, but art gallery lady is gonna get a helluva surprise when she receives that rate sheet, because wait a minute …

"My friend Sharon mentioned that your business was new, so you did her event for free to gain experience."

The bottom line is that art gallery lady is gonna be pissed if she has to pay for something that Sharon got for FREE. Chances are, she'll move on and find some other "newbie" who hasn't read this book who will do it for free … But, baby, that's cool, let her go – you don't need that shit. You're a Matriarch and you are to be paid your worth!

In the end, all that hard work Kimberly put in hoping to get access to Sharon's hot list of contacts didn't pay off. Instead she tainted her new brand with the "works-for-free" stigma.

So how will Kimberly bounce back from this? She may not. Anyone who has ever started a business knows that the last thing you can afford to do in the beginning is give away your services. Kimberly has inadvertently set her prices as *free*, and it's gonna to be really hard for her to start charging what she's worth now that she's set this tone. Her talent, her dependability, her artistry, her compassion, and her ability to capture every special moment of a life event is overshadowed by the fact that she didn't value her own expertise …

IF I DON'T TAKE THIS FREE JOB, I MIGHT MISS OUT ON OTHER PAID OPPORTUNITIES

Free work leading to paid work is a myth. You should never give your services away for free and expect that this act will result in well-paid work. The next time someone tries to convince you that it's "worth it" for you to provide free catering or free marketing copy for a website, stand your ground. Insist on being paid your standard fee or walk … A Matriarch does not miss out on "opportunities" when she rightfully says NO to someone who does not appreciate her time and abilities. It's actually the other way around.

You could miss out on PAID work if you're busy designing some chick's wedding invitations pro bono. Don't miss out on paid work because you're too busy doing FREE work …

WORKING FOR FREE DESTROYS YOUR INDUSTRY

On a regular basis I watch strong, passionate, dedicated doulas work themselves right out of their rewarding career. Many doulas are drawn to birth work because birth is empowering and meaningful and they have a desire to help other women experience it positively. Helping a laboring woman find her inner strength, being present the moment she transitions into becoming a mother, is profound and impactful work. But if you don't get paid, #1, it's a hobby, and #2, it's not sustainable.

I can tell you firsthand that being a doula is endlessly inspiring, but it's also hard work and exhausting. As women who have had babies know, labor and birth are unpredictable, and that means a doula's entire life is unpredictable. Many nights I fell into bed, only to be woken up a short time later by a client who needed me. I could be in the middle of preparing dinner or doing homework with my kids when the call came that a client was in labor. That call could take me away from my own family for a few hours, but in many cases, it was as many as 12 hours or longer, occasionally even multiple days.

Once I committed to a client, I was there for the long haul, supporting her in every imaginable way. Now, as a Matriarch, my self-esteem was intact, and I knew my worth. I was well compensated for the exceptional service I was providing. My contract clearly stated my fees, and I was paid more if a birth went beyond 12 hours. My clients received the support they needed, and I made enough money to be a strong contributor to my household.

This arrangement seems like a no-brainer, right? But other parts of the doula world didn't see things the same way I did.

Believe it or not, some doula training organizations encourage or insist that doulas attend births without payment or work on a sliding scale to support a vision that "every woman deserves a doula." But what does the doula deserve? Interestingly enough, they don't think that doula training should be free. They seem to be charging their worth but not paying that message forward.

Anyway, this means that a doula could be away from her family for a ridiculous amount of time, leaning on family members or friends for childcare, or paying for it with money they're not even earning. They'll pay out of pocket for gas, parking, and meals for the duration of the labor, and they will follow up a few days later with another FREE in-person meeting.

I know firsthand that the work doulas do is important. I've certainly seen how having the support of a doula can improve a person's birth experience. I'm also well aware that plenty of fierce pregnant women do this birth thing without a doula and get along just fine on their own, thank you very much.

WHEN YOU WORK FOR FREE, OTHER WOMEN ARE EXPECTED TO DO IT TOO, AND THAT JUST SUCKS

I don't think that attending the birth of every woman in America falls on my shoulders, or the shoulders of doulas in general – especially if it means they can't afford to pay their rent, put gas in their cars, or food on their tables. The idea that women deserve a good birth experience doesn't mean that a doula is required to provide one at a cost that is detrimental to her and her family and, ultimately, her entire industry.

When there is an expectation that doulas will work for free or next to nothing, there is a wider expectation that if you want to hire a doula, all you'll have to do is hand over some spare change, a basket of eggs, or a granola bar and a bottle of water ... And there goes an entire industry because ... who the fuck can pay their mortgage with a dozen eggs?

Creating an expectation that women should put in such long, hard hours and not be compensated is ridiculously misguided and results in doulas leaving the industry and the work they love because they can't afford to do it.

Listen, it doesn't matter if you're a doula, an acupuncturist, a landscaper, or a writer. When you work for free, you're setting an expectation. And that expectation is that work in your industry does not have enough value to warrant compensation. The moment you say, "Yeah I'll write that copy for your new website," you're actually making it harder for women throughout your field to demand the compensation they deserve. If the expectation becomes "Writers love what they do so much that they'll do it for free," that's going to leave you struggling in an industry where it's nearly impossible to reap the benefits of your hard work, education, and investment of time. Every time you charge your worth for the services you're providing, you are paving the way for others in your field to do the same.

Don't Make Another Woman's Career Your Hobby

I work with women who come from all different backgrounds. Some of them are single mothers who have scrimped and saved and busted their asses to train as doulas. Others come to us from a place of financial privilege.

But stick with me for a minute on this ... what if the woman of privilege decides she'll attend four or five births a year, and since the money doesn't matter to her, she'll charge just $250 a birth to cover her "expenses." After all, women *need* doulas in order to have babies, right (cups hands, pretends to sneeze, and says, "bullshit") ...

But hang on a second, what about that single mom who is planning to charge the going rate of $1,200 for a birth, which btw, is what she needs in order to pay her rent, buy clothes for her daughter, and cover her childcare expenses. Who are people going to hire when it comes down to price? Yeah, exactly. The $250 doula.

When a Matriarch sets her rate, it isn't just about her – it's about every other woman out there who is working hard to earn a living. So, if you're blessed with the good fortune of not needing money and you're thinking about dabbling in an industry (especially a female-dominated one), think twice before you arbitrarily set your rates. Making another woman's career your hobby has bigger implications than you even know.

I'M IN TRAINING; THAT'S WHY I'M NOT CHARGING

Let's talk about what it really means to be "in training." Sure, training is a thing that happens. When a pilot is learning to fly a plane, her teacher or trainer is in the next seat – providing guidance and expertise and keeping her from crashing onto a crowded highway. Surgeons aren't given a scalpel, told "good luck," and sent into the operating room to remove some poor dude's spleen. They are guided and trained by someone with years of experience. But, at some point in time, the training is OVER. The individual is deemed ready to fly a plane, remove internal organs, or whatever it is they have been trained to do. If you have completed the necessary training to do your job, you are TRAINED. You are no longer *in training*, and you shouldn't accept pay that is anything other than what a professional in your field rightly deserves.

WORKING FOR FREE IS YOUR FAMILY'S SACRIFICE

My family really enjoys my company and, I think it's safe to say, yours does too. So, make sure whatever takes you away from them is worth their while. My business was growing, and I was working hard. My business partner, Debbie, and I were attending births, handling all of the administrative tasks, and booking client meetings that would sometimes run past 8:00 at night. One particular night, we were with a client doing a prenatal visit to discuss her hopes and plans for her upcoming birth. My purse was sitting next to me, and I could hear the ping of a text message. Then another. I finally took a moment to look. It was a text message from my daughter. It was by no means an emergency of gargantuan proportions, but in her 13-year-old mind she was having a crisis.

The text said: "Mom. My hair looks like shit! Can you come home, and blow dry it for me??!!! Please!!!!"

Moments later Debbie's phone starts ringing. She sees it's her son, and she politely excuses herself to take the call in another room. When we were finished with the meeting, I asked if everything was OK. She said her son right that second absolutely needed to tell her that he just learned "that Grandpa's friend was in the mafia."

My point with this is that sure, we were hustling – building a business, supporting birthing families, and making money, but the bottom line is that it was 8:00 at night, and our families wanted us home. These may sound like small sacrifices, and certainly every working mom has missed something at one time or another, but when it happens over and over again, it starts to add up.

I hate the idea of a Matriarch missing out on seeing her daughter play Tinkerbell in the school play because she agreed to attend a woman's birth for free. I can't stand the idea of a Matriarch missing her son's first steps because she was busy staging someone else's home for resale for free. Be deliberate about what moments you are present or not present for, and make sure that if you're missing out on family time, you're being well compensated.

Calling All Matriarchs! Viva la Revolution!

The revolution begins now and all you have to do is boldly insist.

There was a time when it became clear to me that the industry that I love and had worked tirelessly in for more than a decade needed to be revolutionized. As I've said, doulas and birth workers as a whole lacked sustainable practices, with giving away their services for free being the leading unsustainable practice. Things have begun to change now in the doula industry, and they are continuing to improve. I'm proud to have played a role in that change.

But a revolution of this magnitude does not come without pushing up your sleeves and going into battle. When you decide that enough is enough and that you can no longer work for free, your "colleagues," your "friends," your "comrades," will turn on you. They will call you a money-hungry bitch. They will say that all you care about is money and not your clients. They will question your passion and they will literally work to destroy your esteem. They will bully you and they may leave you questioning your decision.

But you've got to ask yourself why: Why are they so offended by you charging your worth? How does it impact them? Why do they care, and why are they so angry? I'll tell you why. Because they know damn well that they should do it too and they don't know the first thing about how. They will literally fight to defend their right to work for free.

They'll even get creative about it. They say things like, "I take 10% from all of my paying clients to build a 'fund' for clients who can't afford me ..." What the Fuck Are You Talking About?!?!?! Why should client A pay for client B to have your services ... That's not fair, nor is it ethical.

Look, I know how capable you are, and I know that when you start demanding the rate you deserve for your expertise, it'll be not only empowering—but life changing. You'll also be building a bridge, making it easier for other women to charge their worth too! Any idea how good that's going to feel to you?

THREE FEARS PREVENTING US FROM CHARGING OUR WORTH AND REACHING OUR FULL POTENTIAL

Here's the deal, we're all afraid of something. Even the most fierce Matriarch of them all feels the stranglehold of fear from time to time. But what she does with that fear, and what she does once she recognizes that it's *just* fear, is what determines the trajectory of her life or circumstance.

Sometimes, in life's darkest moments, she begins to believe the insidious messages that fear sends her. You know ... self-doubt, unworthy, undeserving, etc.

She starts to think "I can't charge $1,200 per birth, I'm not worth $1,200 ... I just started doing this!" Or, "Why should anyone hire *me* to make their wedding cake? I've only made a couple. Maybe I should do a few for free to build my portfolio."

I know you've had these thoughts. Most of us have at one point or another. I know it's the mindfuck called fear that got you there, but, girl, we gotta get you out, and I'm coming in to get you.

Let's grab these fears by their mean-spirited, lying, manipulating, contriving-ass throats and end their tormenting wrath. Let's stop them from ever breaking into our spirits and stealing what rightfully belongs to us ever again!

Fear #1 Impostor Syndrome

> *"I can't charge for my services because I'm brand new. I don't have enough experience to charge. I'm not worthy of full compensation."*

For some women, it's really difficult to wrap their heads around the fact that classes and training are over and they are fully prepared to serve. You see, they have what's called impostor syndrome – a total brain scam in which an individual fears being exposed as a "fraud" due to their perceived lack of experience and knowledge.

So, look, maybe this is you. Maybe the idea that you are not fully equipped makes you feel unworthy of selling yourself as an expert. And if that's the case, then you'll need some evidence to prove it and I don't believe you have any.

Did you complete your classes? Yes? Did your educator or mentor tell you that you weren't yet worthy of compensation? No? OK! Then you are ready, and it's time to go to work and get paid. Some say that impostor syndrome is deeply rooted in individuals who have strived hard for perfection and have often felt like they came up short.

If impostor syndrome is holding you back, you have to acknowledge it. Once you have, you are going to have to seek out wise counsel to help you get through it. That may come in the form of someone you trust who is in your field and fully understands your education and ability. Sometimes you just have to trust that someone you trust, trusts that you are ready.

In the beginning a little self-doubt is pretty normal. As your confidence grows, your doubt will shrink. But in the meantime, phone a friend and let her lift you up and hold you steady until you can own the expertise that she knows you to have.

Fear #2—Fear of Being Judged

"If I say no, I won't design her website at a discounted rate, she's gonna tell everyone I'm greedy and money hungry."

Sound familiar? This is something I've heard from women all over the world. They are more concerned about being judged than about being able to feed their children. We're judged every day. You know that and I know that. We're judged for what we wear, how much time we spend with our kids, how much we work, what we eat, how much we weigh, and every single decision we make in between. The sooner we free ourselves from caring about what other people think, the sooner we can demand to be paid our worth.

The message that women shouldn't be hungry for money is bullshit. Matriarchs are hungry for many things ... pizza, chocolate, sex, laughter, clothes, beauty, cheeseburgers, and shoes. The list goes on and on. We're not judged for being hungry for any of those things; in fact, most people think it's kind of cute when we mention them. So why is it bad to be hungry for what it takes to buy many of the things on the aforementioned list?

The sooner we realize that being hungry for money isn't dirty and distasteful and relearn that asking for it isn't wrong, rude, or presumptuous, the sooner we will be leading the lives we always wanted.

Money may not solve all our problems, but it certainly does make life easier. And there is something pretty empowering about earning it. It provides for you and your family's needs, it brings a sense of security, and it allows you to have some next level kind of fun. I've lived with it and I've lived without it. And let me tell you, it's much better with it!

Most importantly, your daughters, sisters, nieces, and other young women are watching you. When you charge your worth and don't waiver from your decision to do so, it's a signal to them that they should too. Let's help the next generation see their value, charge their worth, and feel like the Matriarchs we know they are!

Fear # 3—Fear of the Unknown

"This client wants to pay less than I charge, but I think I should do it. I mean, what if I never get another client?"

The fear of the unknown can cause us to do some crazy shit. The list of "what ifs" can spiral out of control and leave us absolutely terrified. If you're not careful, the what ifs will suck out all of that beautiful Matriarchal energy you've been building and leave you feeling worthless and weak. And since we ain't turnin' back now, we gotta plow through this.

Building your own business is hard. It requires endless amounts of energy. Negative energy and thoughts like *What if I never find another client?* or *What if I ask for more money and the client says bad things about me?* are a complete waste of time.

This fear also pops up when a Matriarch takes her business into unchartered territories and is faced with tasks or experiences that are completely new to her. Matriarchs have successfully tackled everything from fourth grade science projects to stretching a meal for four into a meal for seven with no notice. Girl, you know how to spontaneously find a solution in your personal life, and business is no different.

People were fearful that Christopher Columbus was going to fall off the edge of the Earth when he set sail for America. That was fear of the unknown and I think it's human nature to experience it.

We like to be able to anticipate outcomes. If I touch the stove, I'll get burned. That makes sense. I know the outcome: It will hurt, so I don't do it. But when I don't know the outcome and I'm left to my own devices, my mind is all the nourishment fear needs to grow into a mighty beast 100 feet tall.

When that scary bastard rears its ugly head and tells you, "You better take this client for half price; you don't know if there will ever be another one," ask yourself the following questions:

- ◆ "Have I really done everything there is to do to attain clients?"

- ◆ "Have I really put myself out there? Who else can I contact? Who can I meet?"
- ◆ "Have I gone down absolutely every avenue there is that could lead me to more work?"

Women who run out of work have really just run out of marketing strategies. What new direction can you take right now? If your marketing strategy isn't attracting your target demographic, it's time to change that. Take a closer look: Are you expressing your value proposition effectively? Do you need to expand your audience? Can you solve that problem by positioning yourself as an expert and teaching a class or writing a monthly article for a website? The Matriarch that you are won't let you quit until you've exhausted every single possibility.

Understand What "I Can't Pay Your Fee" Really Means

"I didn't get that event planning gig I really wanted; I knew I asked for too much money. I should have lowered my rates."

We've all sent someone our fees, given a quote or a proposal for a job and heard the word, NO. It's just part of being in business. You won't get every job or land every client, and that's fine. It might sting the first time you hear a NO, but listen, that no is totally not about you!

A client choosing to decline your services because he or she doesn't want to pay your fee does not mean you're not worth the price. It doesn't mean you don't do excellent work. And it most certainly does not mean you're charging too much money. When a client declines your services because of what they cost, it really means one of two things: Either you're outside of their budget or they don't feel they deserve the high-quality service you provide.

When I was in my early 20s, I went to a fancy makeup counter in a department store. The woman sat me on a stool and smeared some really awesome ultra-silky lotion all over my face. It felt amazing, and my skin looked like it was about to be entered into a contest for Most Exceptional Looking Skin on

Earth. But at that point in my life, I was strictly a soap-'n'-water kind of girl. I could have afforded one product, but I just didn't see myself as the kind of girl that drops 70 bucks on moisturizer. I wanted to be that lady … but I wasn't.

It didn't mean the product wasn't great and it didn't mean that the woman wasn't great at selling it. It just meant I wasn't gonna buy it. The fancy brand wasn't like "Oh we better lower our prices because this chick thinks soap and water is better." Or "Fuck it! Let's just stop selling cosmetics all together! Let's just give this shit away for FREE."

My point is that, ultimately, you can't let someone else's NO destroy you, your business, or your willingness to continue. I hate to break it to ya, girl, but it's just not about you.

Understand That Luxuries Are Not Necessities and Get OK with It

I'm taking you into some controversial waters here. We've discussed how some people in the birth industry believe that every woman *deserves* a doula. And I've shared with you that there are plenty of women who give birth quite successfully without one. I happen to be one of them. I also know that not every person who would like a doula can afford one. I remember what it's like to struggle financially (cue scene of Randy and Jerry Patterson living outside), but it's not up to me to sacrifice myself and my family so that all women can have doulas.

Food, shelter, water – these are necessities. I am clear on the point that having a doula is a luxury. Having another human being at your beck and call 24 hours a day, 7 days a week, for your support, is a luxury. I provide a luxury service, and I'm okay with that. Statistically, research shows that there are real benefits to having a doula. You should look into it; perhaps you'd like to hire a doula at some point in the future or become one. But the thing is, there is evidence that shows that exclusively eating wholesome organic food has benefits too. No one is dishing out high-quality meals of this nature three times a day because we all *deserve* them.

I think it's incredibly important that we distinguish between what constitutes a luxury and what is a true necessity. There are certainly things that make our lives feel "normal," that many consider necessities. Like that phone that's sitting next to you or the TV that's playing in the background. The electricity that is shining a light on this book while you read it. All very nice, But. Not. Necessities.

If someone can't afford your services right now, it's not really a problem for you to solve.

I'll add a note here that you're still a human being, and so am I. I know the value of education and I am willing to provide it at no cost from time to time to those who truly cannot afford it. The difference is that I do this at a time that is convenient for me. I incorporate it into my schedule and make it available for people who say they want doula support but can't pay. What's interesting is that these scheduled classes typically end up empty. Turns out most people don't value what they don't actually pay for.

GIVING AWAY YOUR SERVICES IS NOT THE SAME AS GIVING BACK TO YOUR COMMUNITY

Giving back to a community that supports you is always awesome. What's cooler than making the world a better place for all of mankind? When my New York–based doula agency reached a certain level of success, my business partner and I determined that we were finally in a good position to start giving back.

We thought about who we'd like to help and what we thought they needed. Since we work with families – families having babies in particular – we decided babies were our people. That is whose lives we wanted to impact most.

As you probably know, diapers are insanely expensive and many families (one in three to be exact) struggle to pay for them. Should I pay the electric bill or buy diapers? Should I buy groceries or diapers? These are not choices any parent should have to make. We founded a 501(c)(3) that focused on diaper need and utilized it to give back to our community. As our business grew, our network did too. That put us in an even better position to collect diapers and get them to families who needed them.

We proudly collected 5,000 diapers that first year. But as we got bigger, we were able to host events in over 20 cities, collecting 500,000 diapers. That's a lot of diapers and a lot less stress for some parents in those communities. That's what helping your community really looks like.

I'm all for a random act of kindness. If you bake your neighbor a pie, then you baked them a pie. If I choose to support a woman who needs my help, I've helped one woman. These are all wonderful things to do, but they do not qualify as giving back to the community. So let's not get ahead of ourselves. One act of kindness is not the same as helping the masses in your community who may be struggling. To be clear, when a woman who does not have her self-esteem intact prioritizes others over herself and gives away her services under the guise of "giving back to the community," she's not actually helping out her community at all. Just think about how much you could really do if you became a huge brand with lots of money and influence.

SERIOUSLY, PLEASE TAKE YOURSELF SERIOUSLY!

"Wow. She takes herself too seriously. Who does she think she is?"

You've heard the digs.

A woman you know has been creating marketing campaigns for local businesses for a few years. At first, it was creating buzz around the opening of a new restaurant. The event was a huge success and it brought her shitloads of new business – a gastropub, a yoga studio, and a bookstore all wanted her help. So what did she do? She rented an office, branded herself as the *best* marketing guru around, and has continued to succeed and grow. Most people are really happy for her. She works hard, and good for her! She chased a dream and brought it to fruition!

But once in a while you'll hear a snarky comment: "We used to hang out, until she started that business. Do you think she still cooks? When is the last time she volunteered at school? I can't remember the last time I saw her ... "

The message that women shouldn't take themselves seriously is seriously ridiculous. If you don't take yourself seriously, who will? Let's turn that message around: Absolutely take yourself seriously. You only reap rewards when you invest in you.

Joy Mangano didn't want to stick her hands in disgusting mop water, and she thought the design of a typical closet hanger was ridiculous. She took herself seriously and is now worth $50 million. Sarah Blakely didn't think she could be the only person out there who wanted underwear that didn't show, smoothed her ass, and made her stomach look flat. It's a good thing she took herself seriously because where would we be without Spanx? And what about Madonna? What if she just thought of herself as a girl who could sing pretty good who liked to cut the fingers off lace gloves for the hell of it? Madonna knew her value, and she demanded her worth.

Whether you see yourself running a small business that you enjoy and that contributes to your household, or you're going to break barriers, dominate, disrupt industries, and be worth billions, it's totally up to you. Whatever it is you want, you deserve it, you can get it, and it all starts by knowing and charging your worth.

The Matriarch Code of Conduct: Don't Ask for Free Shit and Don't Take Free Shit

Ideally, this goes without saying. I mean, we've all agreed that we want to be paid, and paid well for our expertise, time, and services right? RIGHT. That being said, do not, under any circumstances, ASK other women to give you shit for free. Don't be a SHARON – asking for free services in exchange for "spreading the word."

In order for women of all walks of life to get comfortable charging what they're worth – we need to stop asking each other for free stuff, period. Money is not bad. NOT having money is what's bad. And the reluctance between women to exchange actual money for services must stop now.

Chapter 6

A Life and Business That's Carefully Crafted

I want to tell you about a really valuable skill set you have but that you might be fumbling around with.

You may not realize this, but every Matriarch has experience in "brand development." People pay experts tens of thousands of dollars for brand development services and you, my friend, DIY'd it! Now, while you have in fact done this yourself, I'm not quite sure you were strategic or deliberate about it. But the good news is, it's not too late to change that!

Let me explain. Branding is the practice of strategically building a company's value proposition and reputation. A value proposition is a cleverly designed description of how your product or service is uniquely superior to other brands who sell similar things. A brand's reputation is based on the quality of its products or services, how it makes others feel, how it interacts, how it behaves, what it stands for and believes in, and whether or not it is aesthetically pleasing.

Being deliberate about creating your brand allows you to thoughtfully consider what you want to be known for. Once you know what that is, you can work backward from there to establish it. A Matriarch doesn't just hope for the best, she consciously designs her brand and she is perceived the way she intends to be.

A brand's message is conveyed in a multitude of ways, and whether it's business branding or personal branding, it should always be done purposefully.

Branding: Just Do It

Let's look at a brand like Nike. Nike is an American multinational corporation. They are the world's largest supplier and manufacturer of athletic shoes, apparel, and other sports equipment. The name itself originates from Greek Mythology. "Nike" was the Goddess of speed, strength, and victory. That's kind of sexy if you ask me.

But let's focus on their tagline for a minute since it's so iconic and speaks so loudly to the person Nike hopes to attract. Nike tells us to, "Just Do It." It's an anchor in their brand's message. It ties us as consumers to the brand. Nike seeks to attract athletes, right? And athletes don't whine and complain. They … Just Do It. The brand makes sense to the person Nike seeks to attract; it speaks their language.

But even wiser, Nike knows that with this message, they will also attract those who *want to* … Just Do It. Expressing this brand message so clearly to the world has been a key element to the company's success. Add to it exceptional customer service, a comfortable price point, and positive messaging that supports this kick-ass tagline, and we have ourselves an athletic brand of great speed and incredible strength that is victorious in the marketplace!

Nike cleverly tied this message to an onomatopoeia; *Swoosh*. Their logo alone, the iconic Swoosh symbol, intentionally inspires movement, and stimulates the message of get up and go. Or simply put … Just Do It.

People Are Their Own Brands

The interactions we have with other people convey messages about who we are. And while we are not businesses (we are individual people) and those we interact with are not customers (they are neighbors, family members, friends, and acquaintances), we are making an impression on them. That impression will empower their decision to keep us around or kick us to the curb. I'd like to be kept around.

Clearly, there are parallels between building a personal brand, and a business building its brand.

IT SETS US APART

Branding is important because it's how we define what is unique about us. It's what differentiates us from others and it's what enables people to know what they can expect from us. It helps them anticipate how we will respond or react; it's how we become predictable in the minds of others. When we are somewhat predictable, people feel safer connecting with us.

MEET THE ROCK 'N' ROLL DOULA

I'll use myself as an example. I love rock 'n' roll. My whole life, rock 'n' roll has been playing in the background. As a small child, I remember going to festivals with my hippie parents. I was maybe six or seven years old. I'd be wearing cut-off shorts and my mom would take a red bandana, fold it into a triangle and tie it around me as a shirt. My dad made braided leather headbands and my long curly hair would be parted in the middle and flowing freely with one of those headbands across my forehead and tied around the back of my head. The spirit of rock 'n' roll filled my soul.

My family was involved in the music business. My aunt and uncle opened a record store in the early 1980s and, soon after, started managing some heavy metal bands. I found myself as a 14-year-old girl in the company of bands like Metallica and Anthrax on a pretty regular basis. My parents got involved and were responsible for the arts and graphics for some pretty legendary album covers. Every weekend was a different show at a different venue, and it was not uncommon for them to take me out of school on a Friday to go help set up for an event. Music has always been a priority and it is a deeply rooted part of who I am.

As my life evolved and I became a doula, it wasn't long before I took on the persona of the "Rock 'n' Roll Doula." The Rock 'n' Roll Doula is my personal brand. It encompasses everything I stand for and believe in. The rock 'n' roll attitude is one of rebellion, freedom: it's having a fierce presence without fear of judgment. It's emotional and real and it's worn on the sleeve of a black leather jacket.

As a doula, I enable the empowerment that comes with the rock 'n' roll spirit in the clients that I work with. I help them face their fears and find their fierce. My personal brand speaks loudly and clearly. You can see it when you look at me and you can feel it in my space. I breathe it into others the way Robert Plant did (look him up) when he stepped up to the mic.

NOW, MEET YOURSELF

It's your turn! Over the next couple of days, I want you to ask the people in your life to describe you. Ask specifically what they would say about you if they were describing you to someone else. Encourage them to move quickly past the part about your height, weight, and hair color, and get to the good stuff: how they describe your personality. What character traits stand out to them. What they would say you rally for or believe in. Don't lead them. Just keep saying, "Tell me more." As a self-awareness exercise, you should also take some time to write down what you anticipate them saying. See if you're accurate about how you are perceived.

Now, you may hear what those people say and think, yes, that is exactly what I intend for people to think of me. It may define you to a T and you may be super proud of yourself at the end of the exercise. If that's the case, that's awesome and this next section won't apply to you.

But if you found a big disconnect between what they said about you and what you expected, or what you hoped they would say, well, then you've got some work to do, and I'm gonna help you. I'll show you exactly how to create a personal brand that connects who you are on the outside to the extraordinary Matriarch on the inside who's just dying to get out!

Rebuilding Your Brand Based on Your Authentic Self

Ok, so you did my little exercise and what you found is that what others likely perceive about you is nothing like who you actually are, or what you necessarily want associated with your brand.

Maybe what you heard was something like, "She's really nice; sweet. She prioritizes others but always seems a bit frazzled. She's always in a hurry but will stop and chat for hours. She volunteers a ton of time but says she can't afford to participate in events that cost money. She loves her family but is sarcastic when talking about them ... "

Maybe after hearing this, you decide ... Wait a minute! That's not the impression I want people to have of me.

Well, girl, don't worry! A Matriarch starts anew. She leaves the past behind her and she recognizes each day as an opportunity to lead the life she always wanted. So if you are not pleased, you will simply take a new action. Let's get started on that now.

This *deliberate* brand that you are about to build is to only be based on *your authentic* self. Do you understand me? That means you will have to release yourself of the chains that have been placed on you by the expectations of others, now and in the past. You will have to give yourself permission to mentally tell those people to fuck off and break out of the box they have placed you in. That's not gonna be easy because their voices have been cultivating you and shaping you your whole life. But today, you take that power back.

You're gonna have to dig deep and find the authentic voice that lives within you. The one that the people in your life have been trying to silence by telling you to be more like this or more like that. Less of this and less of that ... Girl, let me be clear, no matter how loud those voices are or have been in the past, no matter what direction they come at you from, they can never remove who you actually are deep down inside.

So let's not concern ourselves with what others think we should be, or what they express they want for us, and instead, focus on bringing exactly who we are to the surface.

SCHEDULE YOUR DISCOVERY SESSION NOW!

A discovery session is a brainstorming opportunity to design and develop a solid "image" for a brand. In this case, I am encouraging you to use it as a personal-evaluation process to create a clear interpretation of who you are. This will help you to become more comfortable in your own skin and give others an accurate perception of you. It will also lead you to personal fulfillment, which happens to be the real prize you're after here anyway, my friend.

Keep in mind that the reason this is so important is because if you don't express who you authentically are and what your true message is, you will seem less impressive than you actually are. By not giving others the opportunity to know your true self, you are removing the chances of them falling wildly in love with you.

The world wants to know who the fuck you are. So take some history changing actions that give them that opportunity, OK?!

Do this by yourself or work together with some other soon-to-be-Matriarchs. By the way, if you choose the latter, wine and chocolate will enhance this experience immensely. You may also want to have a box of tissues handy. Just sayin'.

Let's begin. Allow yourself to read deep into the following questions while *feeling* the thoughts and emotions they each inspire. How you feel as you explore your responses is more valuable than what you think. Thus, the reason for the tissues.

WHAT MATTERS MOST TO YOU?

What thoughts never seem to go away for you? If you continuously focus on education, perhaps personal growth is something that matters most to you. Ask yourself what you fear most. When you fear losing someone, it is a clear indication that that person really matters to you. If you have trouble sorting out the things that matter most to you, explore some of your fears and ask yourself why you fear them. What would you regret not doing or investing in?

What Worries You?

What, if anything, keeps you up at night with worry? Is it related to finances? Health? Relationships? Age? Work? This is closely related to what matters most to you and getting to the bottom of it will really give you a direction for your energy and focus.

What, If Anything, Are You Passionate About?

What do you constantly read, research, and talk about? If you were given the world's microphone for 60 seconds, what message would you want to convey right now? I say "right now" because this can change. What we are passionate about in our 20s verses our 50s may be different. In fact, it likely will be. Today, focus on today, OK? What would you be doing today if you could be doing absolutely anything in the world?

If this question has you stumped, you may want to start broadening your horizons. Do this by first searching the back corners of your mind for something in your past that you loved. Maybe as a child you had an experience that was amazing and your passion lies somewhere within that experience. If your memories still leave you without a direction, take a class. Join a club. Try something new. You could be missing out on something you might really enjoy.

How Do You Want Other People to Feel after Spending Time in Your Presence?

This question is here because you have a choice about how people feel after interacting with you and what they walk away with is part of your brand message. How do you want them to feel? What three adjectives do you want them to use to describe you? You can start by thinking about opposites. Here are some examples: radical or conservative, serious or silly, curious or cautious, organized or careless, cooperative or difficult, energetic or lazy, bold or timid. The list goes on and on.

For each comparison, consider all of the in-betweens. It doesn't have to be an extreme. Perhaps it's a varying degree of one or the other that may best describe you. Do this exercise to determine what adjectives you would feel proud to be associated with.

WHAT ARE SOME OF THE PARTICULAR PRINCIPLES THAT YOU STAND FOR AND BELIEVE IN?

For the purpose of answering this question, I want you to imagine that you have a high-powered position with a very well-known company doing something you absolutely love. Imagine that your salary is upward of $250,000 a year and your benefit package is over-the-top. OK, got it?

Now ask yourself what could happen within this company or what action could this company take that would cause you to walk away from it all. Take your time with this; really think it through. This thought process when done with diligence will likely trigger some emotion. Allow that to happen and use it to affirm your belief system.

WHAT ARE THE BENEFITS THAT YOUR FRIENDSHIP OFFERS OTHERS?

Are you a good friend? What do you bring to friendship? Don't slip into listing the features of your friendship: "I'm really nice, I'm reliable, I show up." Instead, get to how your friendship benefits someone else.

Here's an example. I don't know if it applies in your case, but it's a starting point for your exploration. "People benefit from my friendship because I make them a priority. I actively listen to them and work hard to be objective."

WHERE DO YOU SEE YOURSELF IN 10 YEARS?

This will lead you to creating a vision for your future. I mean, shit, the future is inevitably coming so we might as well have a plan in place, right? Your answer to this question will enable you to see the bigger picture and will help you in creating habits and behaviors that become part of the identity that gets you where you want to be.

WHAT BELIEFS OR PRINCIPLES ARE YOU WILLING TO FIGHT FOR?

First, by "fight" I don't mean like an earrings off, hair in a ponytail, hold my jacket, I'm about to kick this bitch's ass, kind of fight.

What I'm getting at is that when someone threatens or assertively challenges your core values or principles, something deep within you takes over and your adrenaline kicks in. I want you to figure out what core values or principles being challenged would evoke this reaction for you.

WHAT KINDS OF COMPLIMENTS WOULD YOU LIKE TO RECEIVE?

While we should never place too much focus on what others think of us, when we are defining ourselves through personal brand development we have the opportunity to behave in a way that brings us the result we are looking for.

So I ask, what do you want people to say about you? What would be *your* greatest compliment?

Your Brand Aesthetic: Are You Bland or On Brand?

So that was the first step. And it was a pretty gnarly step at that. Hopefully you took a lot away from it and learned a great deal about yourself.

Now we have to think about this brand's aesthetic. What does it look like? In business branding, the next step would be to start designing a logo, choosing fonts, and picking colors. But you are not a business; you are a person. So in this case, we're gonna focus on your personal appearance and how it connects you to your brand identity.

If we learned that your brand is outgoing and sassy with a splash of feminist views, a dash of higher education, and a pinch of yogi, would I know that from looking at you? Would I see you at a yoga class and think, "Wow, there's something about this chick. I want more of her in my life." Or would I inadvertently not notice you and miss out on what could have been an incredible friend opportunity? The question really is, are you bland or are you on brand?

Part of being carefully crafted is adorning yourself in a way that aligns with who you are. But you must also consider that part of feeling and conveying confidence is looking like the best version of who you are.

If you're smart, do you look smart? If you love nature and the great outdoors, does it show up in your personal appearance?

Your clothes? The car you drive? The bag you carry? What message is your personal appearance conveying? Now don't confuse this with simple vanity. This is about conveying a strong and authentic message about who you are. This is not about being vain or shallow. It is actually quite deep and identifying.

Now that you have a clearer understanding of your brand, when you are out shopping and you see something and think, hmmm ... that's cute. Stop for a moment and think to yourself, does this item represent *me*? The me that I am on the inside and the me that I want others to see? Is this something that will contribute to defining my brand?

You can recognize something as cute and think, that screams "Debbie's brand," but if it doesn't even whisper yours, either leave it on the rack or buy it for Debbie.

I'm not saying you have to go spend thousands of dollars on a new wardrobe or buy yourself the most expensive haircut in town. You don't have to go buy a new car or get a new bag. I mean if you want to, I'm certainly not going to be the one to stop you, but don't misunderstand what I'm saying here.

All I want is for you to be deliberate about it when you do. When you go buy a new shirt, buy one that looks like a smart, sassy, outdoorsy yogi would wear it. They come in all price points so there is no reason for you not to. Not quite sure how to choose one? There's a resource for that, Matriarch. We call it, Pinterest!

STEP UP TO THE MIC

The next question is, what is this brand's voice? As the Rock 'n' Roll Doula, my words are powerful and fierce – sometimes a bit shocking and rebellious (as you may have noticed) – but also empowering and uplifting. Rock 'n' roll is edgy, and my brand's voice speaks that.

Let's look at a different brand's voice. Take the Demur Doctor. She's polished and crisp. She's playful but sophisticated. She's prompt and courteous. She's cautiously adventurous, careful, and calculated. And for these reasons, she speaks slowly and meticulously. She's conscientious and thorough in her explanations, always asking specifically about each member of a friend's family and following up on the events in each of their lives. She remembers important things with astounding detail. She is authentic and that is evident to others.

Take a mental pause from time to time and ask yourself if your words and tone are really yours. Are you mimicking others, or are you being authentic to your own brand's voice? You can be inspired by others, and likely will be, but remember to stay true to yourself.

Whatever you do, just be careful you're not trying to morph into that cool chick in the corner sipping a latte. What you see as cool about her is a whole package; it's an entire brand. You can't just slap the same badass hat on your head that she's wearing and share her cool. You'll look like an asshole. It's not the hat that's making her cool; it's the confidence she walks in when she wears it. She's confident because she built an authentic brand, and that hat is just part of its aesthetic.

Martinis, Ski Resorts, and Douchebags: How NOT to Find Yourself

Don't take any of this lightly. This is a powerful personal exercise and doing it will enable you to have a deeper understanding of how to build a business brand now or in the future. If you don't take care of this now, it could seriously fuck you up later.

Have you ever met someone who hasn't ever sorted this stuff out? I bet you have. She's the woman that ends up feeling absolutely desperate to "find herself," which leads to her insatiable need to run: to go and "search for who she is."

When a woman makes a decision to leave her partner and her kids out of desperation, thinking it's how she will find herself, she accepts reckless abandon as her next step. Imagine the desperation associated with that decision. It comes from letting life just happen to you.

What the fuck?! You're going to Maine to sit in a ski lodge and drink a martini with some douchebag because you need someone to tell you you're pretty and you need to feel alive again? You will never feel more alive than when you're living in your truest and most authentic self, and I am here to tell you that that is not at a ski lodge with some douchebag drinking a martini.

Girl, I don't want you to find yourself there, and I don't think you do either. In fact, that is how you lose yourself, NOT find yourself.

Your Personal Style Guide

Let me show you how this branding thing worked for a woman named Rachael. Rachael and I were working to create her business's brand, but I suggested that we start with her personal brand first. I knew that before she could really step into this entrepreneurial role, she had to understand and embody the fullness of her own personal brand.

Individual people run small businesses, and a personal brand matters to the success of any small business.

I could see Rachael's brand a mile away, but she hadn't seen it and she certainly hadn't learned to bring it to life yet. She hired me as her "wise counsel" to basically spray the Windex on the window into herself and wipe it clean so that she could clearly see what she was missing.

What Rachael needed to develop was "a personal style guide" that would give her a reference point for clarity and for making decisions that would enable brand alignment. Here are some things you should know about Racheal. She's earthy. She's deliberate. She chooses every word with precision. She can see inside the mind and soul of the people around her and then put those insights into crystal clear words.

She uses words to lift others up. She chooses hygiene products based on ingredients and always has her nose in a book. She goes nowhere without her leather-bound journal and a pen in every pocket of her low-hanging hip bag. When she's dressed in a flowing pair of patterned palazzo pants with a silk blouse billowing out from under a smart-fitted, tan suede blazer with the sleeves rolled up, all of her gorgeous characteristics are amplified.

When I said the words, "Rachael, you are the Boho Brainiac!" her eyes got wide, her mouth dropped open, and suddenly it all became clear. Just like I'm the Rock 'n' Roll doula – or wife, or mother, or CEO, or business coach, or author – basically, anything I do, I do as the Rock 'n' Roll [woman] … Rachael is the Boho Brainiac [fill in the blank].

WHAT IS YOUR TITLE? AND WHAT STYLE GUIDE GOES WITH IT?

Your branding keeps you on track. It helps you make decisions that are so clear to you that they can become just as clear to your acquaintances or customers. People begin to trust you, and your authenticity is what leads the way.

As you start doing this, your brand will evolve, and this thinking will eventually become second nature. You'll find yourself referencing your Personal Style Guide less and less because your intuition will take the wheel and will never steer you in the wrong direction again.

Your Family Has Also Been Branded

Understanding and developing your personal brand was only the beginning. You, in all of your infinite wisdom or lack thereof, also created a family brand. That is, if you've in fact started a family. The best way I can explain this is by introducing you to the Duchants.

Marie Duchant is a painter and graphic designer. Her husband Charles is an architect, and together they have created the most beautiful, culturally rich home in the neighborhood. A party at the Duchant home is an event that no one is too busy for. You know when you arrive that you'll be treated to great music and artistically decadent food, and you'll be in the presence of inspiring and intellectual people.

Their three sons will be there, pulling out chairs for guests, refreshing drinks, and engaging soulfully in adult conversation. Before the night is through, Miles, their oldest, will captivate partygoers with an original composition on their hand-painted, antique upright Steinway.

You will leave feeling inspired and somehow smarter and more cultured. In fact, the Duchants have this effect on everyone they meet. But if you ran into Marie Duchant on the street and asked her to describe her "family's brand," she would likely say, "Brand? We don't have a brand."

The truth is, it's unlikely that Charles and Marie ever sat down to intentionally craft a brand that exudes culture, excellence, and intellect. It's also unlikely that they showed their three boys a PowerPoint presentation on how to be chivalrous and engaging and how to behave in a manner that is in line with their family's brand identity.

The Duchants simply lived in authenticity, and because they did, the family brand that evolved defined them and set them apart from others. And that's exactly what makes a business's brand powerful. It defines the business and sets it apart in their industry. It makes visible their value proposition and it attracts their target market (we'll get to what that means in a minute).

When I start to talk about branding in my business classes, most of the people think we're going to talk about logos, colors, and fonts. They're very surprised when I say that comes a bit later.

But let's look at another example.

The Wedding Therapist: Finding the Starting Point for Her Business's Brand

Glynna grew up in a small town in Texas. She is married to Robert, who is an engineer for a company that manufactures airplane engines. Glynna owns a booming wedding planning business. She's sought after, feverishly referred to, and her name alone says "the perfect wedding" in the small town where she's lived her whole life. Her entire business began when she planned her best friend's wedding right out of high school. The photos of that event moved quickly through social media and her phone started ringing. "I heard you planned Arianna's wedding. Can you help with mine?" And from there, Glynna built a business based on customer need that grew to four full-time employees and a calendar booked more than a year in advance.

That was until Robert got an offer he couldn't refuse, to transfer to the West Coast making nearly double his current salary. Glynna's whole business revolved around her location. She has an incredible skill set, but her clients came exclusively from word of mouth. The idea of moving to a new area, where her business had no reputation yet, left her paralyzed. So as any good Matriarch would do, Glynna sought wise counsel.

She was desperate to take her experience and expertise with her to the West Coast, where she'd have to start from the beginning and wasn't sure how.

The first thing I helped her do was write a business plan because she needed a road map to get to her business's final destination. Part of writing a business plan is, of course, brand development, and I was excited to tackle that with her.

Glynna understood that her client base in Texas came from her personal connections and referrals, not from deliberately building a brand, marketing it, and attracting clients. She recognized that she had no personal connections where she'd be on the West Coast and that, without them, referrals would be nonexistent. She was confident that once she landed her first client, more would follow, but she also knew that people planning weddings don't walk around in white gowns with signs around their necks that say, "Hey, help me plan my wedding."

What Glynna needed to do was define who she wanted to serve and build a brand that would attract them. To this Matriarch's advantage, she knew who these people were, inside and out. She knew what gender they were, how old they were, and what mattered most to them. She knew what social media platforms they were seeking inspiration from, and she knew what magazines they were reading. She knew how to ask the right questions to help them develop a vision for their wedding.

People in her town called her "the wedding therapist." She could get into the head of a bride and pull out her wildest dreams. She had a stop-at-nothing attitude about bringing a woman's biggest wedding wishes to fruition. Whether it was a Cinderella fairy-tale wedding or a sacred campground ceremony, Glynna could create it with style and perfection.

As she and I worked through the branding part of her business plan, the words practically jumped off the paper. Glynna's value proposition as a wedding planner is her ability to bring a fantasy to reality. When I spoke those words to her, her face lit up. It was just like the moment when Rachael realized she was in fact the Boho Brainiac.

At that very moment, "Once Upon a Wedding—Bringing Your Fantasy Wedding to Fruition" was conceptualized. The tagline spoke directly to the target demographic Glynna wanted to serve, in exactly their language.

Now Glynna had a starting point, and around this she could easily build a style guide. She could build a website and marketing materials that would attract the clients she wanted to serve. She could now start meeting with the graphic designer who would develop the aesthetic of this brand.

A Carefully Crafted Matriarch Business

I should tell you that I never, ever imagined myself as a business owner. The idea of creating and operating a business was never part of who I imagined I'd become, but as my life evolved, so did my passions. If you've never considered it, don't rule it out. It just might mean you haven't gotten to that part of your life yet.

Either way, I hope that by now you can see how being the Matriarch of your life, your home, and your family has prepared you really well for owning a business either now or sometime in the future.

I want you to think carefully about a product or service that you could get excited about selling or providing. Maybe it's hand-crafted soaps or holiday ornaments. Maybe it's baked goods or scented candles. Perhaps you sew, or tutor, or teach dance, or doula, or any number of possibilities that can all become businesses and produce revenue for you.

Now, I want you to think about owning a business around this product or service and who might be interested in buying it.

A Matriarch Knows Her Audience and Crafts a Brand to Suit It

The days of slapping an arbitrary logo on the side of a building and calling it a business are long gone. In this day and age, you must humanize your brand in order to get noticed. Human beings want connection; they want to know who they are contributing to with their hard-earned money. They want to know that you share their values and that you support their causes. And the way they find out is through your brand's message.

While Glynna had history and a reputation in Texas, it wasn't going with her to the West Coast. She'd have to start from the beginning. The thing about branding, when it comes to a new business, is that the business has no history or reputation. It hasn't yet made any decisions, it doesn't have any values, and it can't draw on its authentic self, because it doesn't yet exist.

What's exciting about this is that you get to create it from scratch. Think of it as a lump of clay that you get to mold and shape into a piece of art that you are proud to stamp your name on. If you're the kind of person who gets a paintbrush and is afraid to make art because you think you'll wreck it, seek wise counsel like Glynna did.

Hitting a Bull's-eye

Before you begin branding, you must know who this business of yours seeks to attract. Remember, you started your personal branding process by considering the impression you want to make. In business, it's the same. Only in this case, we seek to make a great impression on a particular audience.

We call them our "target market." A target market is a group of consumers organized by demographics who are the people most likely to desire and purchase your products or services.

When someone is unfamiliar with this term and I introduce it to them, their first reaction is that it seems exclusionary. I get why they think that, so I explain further. To shoot 100 love-potion-filled arrows in 100 different directions and hope that one of them hits "Mr. Right" would be a complete waste of time and resources. Instead, determine what the term "Mr. Right" means to you. Perhaps in this case, it is a man who is extremely handsome, has a great job, a respect for women, is an exceptional communicator, loves to travel, wants two children and a house on the cape, and is intellectually attractive to you. Now, you can take one arrow, fill it with a potent dose of love potion, draw it back, aim with the utmost precision, and launch it directly into the center of the bull's-eye. That is what understanding your target market offers your business.

After working so intimately with so many brides, Glynna had this part in the bag, so she was ready to start with brand development. If you have a business or you are considering starting one, and you haven't clearly identified your target market, that would be step one.

A Matriarch Carefully Crafts Her Target Market and We're Gonna Do That Now

The following questions will lead you to determining who your target market is or would be. Imagine you are looking for one particular person. This person embodies exactly who you believe can afford your product or service and who will benefit most from it. As you move through the following series of thought-provoking questions, imagine how your perfect customer would answer them.

Know the customer and their needs. Who is the person who can benefit most from what you sell? Are they women? Men? Children? Pets? How old are they? Are they in their teens? 20s? 40s? 60s? Where do they live? Which states? Cities? Communities? Neighborhoods? Do they own a home or do they rent? Do they live in an area you are able to serve? What problem are they seeking to fix, or what part of their life do they wish to improve? Can your product or service fix their problem or improve their life?

Know what their personal preferences and lifestyle choices are. Do they avoid chemicals in hygiene products? Do they eat exclusively organic? Are they athletic? When they travel, do they go to the beach? The city? The mountains? Do they stay in the country or travel abroad? Do they have large families or are they single with no children? Is extended family nearby or have they relocated?

Know their interests. Are they animal lovers? Wine drinkers? Foodies? Do they enjoy the outdoors? Hiking? Camping? Are they readers? TV watchers? Podcast listeners? What magazines do they read? What blogs do they follow?

Know where they shop. Apple? Nike? IKEA? Restoration Hardware? Bed Bath & Beyond? Old Navy? Gap? Coach? Michael Kors? Crate and Barrel? BMW? Ford?

Know what social media platforms they engage in. Facebook? Instagram? LinkedIn? YouTube? Snapchat? Twitter? Pinterest?

Know what their values and virtues are. What matters to them? What do they stand for? What do they value? What type of charities do they support? What do they rally for?

Can they afford your product or service? Are they people who are comfortable with investing in themselves? How do they determine something's value? Are they impulsive? Are they "see it, like it, buy it" people? Or are they researchers who determine value through evidence and credibility?

■ ■ ■

When we know the habits of those we seek to attract and we know what they are already attracted to, we can draw on it for inspiration as we build our brand, its aesthetic, and our marketing materials.

Do you see how this exercise can help you determine how to craft a business around your expertise?! You can literally explore your personal skill set and passions, determine if there is a market that will benefit from it, build a business, and go for it!

Chapter 7

Time Management and the Five Rules of Business

I still remember the first time I was hired by a pregnant woman to provide support during her labor and birth. I was so excited to be chosen as the person she would allow into her private, intimate, and vulnerable space. I honestly believe that the only thing more intimate than how a baby gets in a person is how they get out, and I've never lost sight of what an honor it is to be chosen to provide this kind of support. I knew then that I was born to do this kind of work.

I even remember a day where I felt especially grateful and wanted to share how monumental it was for me that I had found my calling. I called my mother and said, "I just want you to know that at least one of your children is doing exactly what she was put here to do." I'm not sure if it mattered to her, but it mattered to me so much that I needed to say it out loud.

The fact that being a doula was my job, that I was paid to do it, and that a business ultimately evolved from it, was thrilling to say the least. To be able to spend your workday focusing on something you are deeply passionate about, as you can imagine, offers a reward like no other.

But this can also get business owners into trouble. When they feel so rewarded by the actual work that they're doing, it is easy to lose sight of the business side of things, like where the next client will come from and the organizational side of entrepreneurship. You see, most people have not figured out a good plan for managing their time during the workday, let alone their personal time, and because of that, they can fail.

Time Management

I ask women at the beginning of my business classes, "How many hours do you invest in the business side of your work per week?" I ask them to raise their hand if they invest at least 5 hours per week in growing their business. Everyone raises their hand. Next, I add 5 hours: "If you invest at least 10 hours in growing your business per week, keep those hands in the air." I increase it by 5 hours as we move along. By the time I get to 25 hours per week, I'm lucky if I have one attendee with a hand left in the air.

Now, if all a business owner ever wants is a part-time paycheck, everything's good and there's no need to continue with the class. But that doesn't seem to be the case. The larger problem is that most entrepreneurs don't have the slightest clue what to do during their workday, so time slips away from them and they feel like shit because their business isn't growing.

The truth is, if and only if you are super deliberate about how you use your time, you can really grow a kick-ass business in less than 40 hours a week! Great news, right? That is, if you only knew exactly what to do when you sat down to "work." Sit tight, my new BFF Matriarch Entrepreneur! We're gonna get to that in a minute!

FACEBOOK, INSTAGRAM, AND PINTEREST, OH MY!

Before you even start your workday, you sabotage it by "checking" your social media accounts … I know you do this because I've been guilty of it too. And whether you realize it or not, you've lost half a morning to videos of four-year-olds playing the drums, photos of your friend's new cat, and the ongoing stalking of your ex-best friend.

Using these platforms may be part of your workday if you are utilizing them for your marketing strategy (which you should be), but, girl, you and I both know that when you start there, it's a procrastination strategy and it cannot be counted as work!

PLANNING AND TRACKING YOUR HOURS

We each get 24 hours every day and what we do with them is entirely up to each of us. My guess is that there's a good chance more of them than you'd like to admit have slipped right through your cell phone–holding hands. And today, you, with my help, put an end to it!

You're about to plan, track, and color code your week.

I'm gonna tell you exactly what to do, but I want you to do it based on what you believe you can do and not what you've been doing. Don't create this based on what you did last week, because last week you were not deliberate about how you used your hours.

TAKE THIS HISTORY–CHANGING ACTION NOW

Either search for or create a seven-day weekly plan sheet. You'll want it to have a column for each of the days of the week and time slots for every hour from 6 a.m. to 10 p.m. Don't tell me "you can't" do this, because we both know that would be a lie ... If you are unsure *how* to do this, use your resources and look it up!

Now for color coding. The following colors represent the activities you will do during the hours you choose for them.

Yellow Yellow will represent personal time. Personal time is when you focus exclusively on you. It is when you shower and get dressed. It is exercise, prayer, meditation. It's reading or writing. It's getting a pedicure or a massage. Yellow represents self-care and it's super important no matter how busy you are.

If you have seven children and work full-time, you're going to have less yellow than a friend with two grown children, but I want to see yellow on that page nonetheless! Every single day of every single week, a Matriarch needs a little bit of yellow. Got it?

Pink Pink represents your relationship (if you are in one). If you are in a relationship, it's because you made a choice to be in it, and when you entered into it, you never imagined it would be last on your list of priorities. And yet, in most cases, I'm pretty sure that that has become the sad truth.

I promise you that if you take your relationship for granted and you don't reinforce your love and your vows with your actions, it will crumble. Being in a relationship (or out of one), should be a deliberate choice. Be deliberate about being in yours.

Green Green represents all activities that produce income. Any hour that you are doing something that can generate income will be represented by the color green. These are your work hours.

Blue Blue represents personal tasks. Personal tasks are very different from the personal time represented by the color yellow.

Personal tasks are all of the things expected of you either by yourself or those who depend on you. They include doctor appointments; pet care; banking; cooking and shopping; laundry; home schooling; driving kids to daycare, dance, soccer, etc.

These are all of the things necessary to keep you and your family moving in a healthy and forward direction.

Purple Purple represents family time. Now here's what's cool about family time. It can stand alone in the form of Sunday dinners, movie nights, board games, picnics, and other awesome activities. And it can also be added into your blue time slots.

You can be doing a personal task like going grocery shopping and the kids can be in the car with you singing songs or sharing stories about their day. The same for folding laundry or cooking a meal. You are a badass multitasker, BUT ...

Purple can ONLY be mixed with blue! It cannot be mixed into the time you've allotted for personal care (yellow), your relationship (pink), or income-producing activities (green). Understood?

Ok, fill it out! Color it in and PRINT IT!!!

Show the People Where They Stand   Show your people where they are on your calendar. Tell them that when the day and time shows purple, you will not be working. When it shows pink, you won't be distracted. When it shows green, everyone better back up because you are generating income for the household. And if that calendar shows yellow, unless their blood is on the outside of their bodies or the house is on fire, they better not even say your name!

Let's Go Make Some Money, Matriarch!

Now that you've figured out your work schedule, we need to break down exactly where you should put your focus when it comes to how to build and grow your business. Providing your services or selling your products goes without saying, but there is so much more that goes into it than that. I've broken your business tasks into five rules for you to work by.

Before I share these rules with you, you should know that I didn't just wake up one day knowing all of this business stuff. As I previously mentioned, I'm a high school dropout with no formal education beyond a high school equivalency diploma. I did this business thing the hard way with one costly mistake after another, every step of the way. It probably would have been easier to quit. But, instead, I dug deep and ultimately got my shit together and figured it all out.

I do, however, remember exactly what it felt like the first time I had to refund a client's money. This particular client hoped to have an unmedicated vaginal delivery. At 38 weeks pregnant, she learned that her baby was breech and that her doctor would be performing a cesarean section. The client decided that she did not want to have a doula support her in this newly introduced scenario (although, doula support for a cesarean section is incredibly valuable), and she asked for a refund. Now, at the time, my contract didn't discuss this and the word "nonrefundable" was not in the contract.

When push came to shove (pun intended), the right thing to do was refund the client's money, and that's what I did. My business was new and giving back that money because of a poorly written contract really hurt.

GROWING PAINS

I made many mistakes as I developed my business, and all of them were completely avoidable. I remember how excited I would get when someone contacted me about doula services. Back then, they would call on the phone. I'd answer the phone and hear the person say, "Hi, I'm looking for a doula and my midwife gave me this number. Is this Randy Patterson?"

Well that's all I needed to hear! My passion would bubble up so high and so fast it was like meeting a new best friend every single time. I would get so engulfed in the conversation that I wouldn't even think to take notes. We would talk about where she was giving birth, what number baby she was pregnant with, how she planned to give birth, what her husband thought about her hiring a doula, and so on and so forth.

By the end of the call, what had transpired could best be described as the beginning of a trusting relationship. Now that's awesome and totally necessary when someone is considering hiring a doula, but what kind of doula do you hire that doesn't even know your name?

I'd have a couple of notes on the back of an envelope that was laying on the kitchen counter. You know, the one the gas and electric bill comes in … I would have scribbled the number 4 on it and a phone number … in crayon …

Hmm … 4? 4th baby? Due on the 4th? The 4th month of the year, April? Why did I write the number 4 …? Great, a phone number and no name … That will make for an awkward call back. "Uhh hi, ummm is this, uhhh … Well, this is Randy, the doula … "

So that was my "client intake call" … What a mess.

Keep in mind that if I was able to take my passion for birth and women and turn it into a successful business with this half-assed "business acumen," then the sky is certainly the limit for you!

Fast-forward many years and many mishaps later, and the answers all seem obvious now. I figured out that there are five rules of business, and since then, I stopped making those costly, reputation-risking mistakes. Each rule includes an overview and it is expected that you will delve deeply into each one. As a Matriarch, I anticipate that you are resourceful enough to find templates, tools, and workshops that support each rule. Perhaps I'll even see you at one of mine one day soon!

Rule #1: It Starts with a Plan

A business plan, that is. A business plan is the "GPS" that takes your business where you want it to go. It prevents you from blindly moving in any and all directions with the "hopes" of an abundant final destination. It enables you to get focused, stay focused, and arrive at your destination quickly and efficiently.

The research and thought that you put into the process of writing a business plan is equally as important as the finished product itself. If you are seeking investors, your business plan will be an essential ingredient in attracting them.

Keep in mind that your business plan is a "living, breathing document" that you will update as your business expands. This is where you will turn first when things aren't going as planned. I encourage small business owners to look back on their business plan when things get a bit "stale" – and then they quickly realize that something has changed.

For instance, if during their competitive analysis (four years ago) they found that there was only one other business in the area that offered similar services, their marketing efforts would be relevant to that small amount of competition. But if in recent years, three other businesses have opened offering similar services in a 30-mile radius, the business will need to revamp its strategy. The business may even need a rebrand in order to gain new traction. Or a new product or service may need to be added to its offerings.

A Plan for Writing a Plan

Sometimes where to begin is the hardest question of all, but in this case, that doesn't really apply. A quick Google search will bring up more options and templates for writing a business plan than you can even count. Look yourself in the eye and repeat after me: "I am not intimidated by writing a business plan. I CAN do this; I WANT to do this; and I WILL do this."

WHAT TO INCLUDE IN THE PLAN

Start with a company description. Who the owners are, what their credentials are, what the legal structure is, and a description of how your product or service benefits the market. Also, include the advantages the business has over its competitors.

You'll incorporate market research and a description of your target market: how you determined their need for your product or services, including statistics, a description of your industry, and the business's projected growth. A detailed evaluation of your competitors, including their strengths and weaknesses, is also necessary.

You'll provide detailed strategies for sales, marketing, and implementation. Include an explanation of how you will promote and market the business. Describe your operational plans. Provide costs of goods and price points. Be sure to include the number of employees or subcontractors you intend to start with and the business's hours of operation.

Engage the support of your accountant to help develop a financial plan for the business. Be prepared with an estimate of all start-up costs, sales projections, and operating costs. Together, determine your accounting and payroll systems and budget. Include this information in your business plan as well as any anticipated needs for additional funding.

EXECUTIVE SUMMARY

This section is the most important part of your business plan if you are seeking investors. While it should be at the forefront of your mind, it is best to write it last, as it summarizes the plan. It should be no more than two pages in length and should be written enthusiastically. It is the first impression your business will have on a potential investor; therefore, it should be designed to entice. Your goal is to get an investor to think, "This is interesting, I want in on this!"

Rule #2: It's Got to Be Legal

You'll need to consider the legal structure of your business and make a decision on what's best for you. This is one of the most important decisions you will make on your business's behalf because of the tax implications. Your legal structure also impacts your personal liability. The options you'll choose from include sole proprietorship, partnership, corporation, S corporation, and limited liability company (LLC). Because of the tax implications, you should seek "wise counsel" in the form of a tax accountant and/or a business attorney.

BUSINESS BANKING

Once you've decided on your legal business structure and have filed the proper paperwork, you will receive the necessary documentation to open a business bank account. Keeping your business's finances separate from your personal finances is a must. Unfortunately, I see many unseasoned entrepreneurs get sloppy about this. I was one myself in my very early days and I know the repercussions first hand. This is a time-consuming, costly, and avoidable mistake. Don't make it!

CONTRACTS

Too many female entrepreneurs fuck this part up. No messing around here. You have to do this right. You don't just pick a friend and be like, "Let's start a business together!" and then open up shop.

You must have a professionally written partnership agreement in place. One of the most important aspects of the agreement is the exit strategy. In other words, when the shit hits the fan and one of you wants out, the exit strategy is what will advise you of the terms.

The best legal advice I ever got about writing one was to pretend I absolutely despised the person I was going into business with. That was difficult because we had become really close friends. When my attorney asked an important question about how I'd want something handled if the partnership ended, I was like, "Oh, she can have that ... I'd be OK with that ... " He said,

"No you wouldn't. You'd be pissed and the contract we are writing right now has to protect you."

What I'm saying here is that unless you are a contract lawyer, don't think you can scribble some terms on the back of a napkin, shake on it, and call it a partnership. It won't work, and I promise you will regret it later. Oh, and it will be incredibly time consuming.

For every service you provide, you must have a contract in place that outlines what the client can expect from you and what you expect from the client. Your fees should be clearly stated, and your refund policy should be included. All of these contracts must be signed by both parties and stored for future reference.

If your business will be engaging the services of subcontractors, you must also have a legal contract in place between them and the business. It should be signed by both parties and safely stored for future reference.

INSURANCE

If you own a business, you need insurance. The purpose of insurance is to help cover the costs associated with any property damage or liability claims. In the event of an incident, paying out of pocket can obliterate a small business. Meet with an insurance broker to determine your business's insurance needs. You will likely be advised to acquire general liability and worker's compensation insurance.

TAXES

In working with your accountant and/or lawyer to set up your business's legal structure, a tax plan is also structured. Allow your accountant to continue to advise you of best practices for being prepared at tax time. Exceptional accounting systems will streamline the process and eliminate confusion during tax prep season for your business.

Your business must seek wise counsel in the form of legal representation, financial planning, and accounting. Expect to have an ongoing relationship with your team of advisors and allow them to handle the necessary tasks to protect you and your business.

Rule #3: It Takes a Systematic Approach

A business without systems in place is a breeding ground for absolute chaos. I had to go back and untangle disasters that could have been avoided with simple operational plans in place, and my goal is to prevent you from having to do the same.

Now, I've learned a lot along the way, but I do not consider myself a master of operations. Because I know this about myself, it means I need ... wait for it ... wise counsel. I need wise counsel in the form of an operations manager or at the very least someone skilled at building and implementing systems.

You will need systems set up that are appropriate for your business: billing, shipping, client communications, and so on. But that's not all. It's totally pointless if you don't have your systems or processes organized in an operations manual.

Let's imagine after three years of running your business solo, you decide to hire an assistant or an office manager. Do you have any idea how long it would take you to explain daily operations: how to do an intake call, process an order, create and send an invoice, add a customer to the database, etc.? It would take weeks or even months for this new employee to have the ability to efficiently do their job.

BUILD AN OPERATIONS MANUAL

As you develop and implement each system, create a document that outlines the process. Keep these documents current and safe in your operations manual. In addition to all of the systems you create, include all logins and passwords to your business accounts, as well as any vendor information that applies.

Keeping this current will contribute to exceptional time management since you won't have to waste time searching for information or personally walking new employees through every detail of each process that pertains to them. Time and money are resources that you don't have enough of to waste.

Rule #4: Marketing Is a Never-ending Process

Marketing is the ongoing process of communicating and educating the consumer about your products or services. This is done while developing a trusting relationship between the consumer and your brand. While this may sound simple, it's certainly not easy.

In the previous chapter, you learned all about brand development based on target market. Marketing is essentially bringing your brand to the market, and now that you have one, you can begin.

There are many strategies when it comes to marketing your business. Some will come more easily for you than others. It is your responsibility to your business to find a combination of ideas that you believe in and develop your annual marketing plan. This is something you will evaluate each year as you plan for the next.

I will define a few strategies for you to start considering.

RELATIONSHIP-BASED MARKETING

This strategy is designed to create a long-lasting relationship with the consumer. Its intention is to build customer loyalty and word-of-mouth referrals. In this day and age, customers want relationships with the brands they become customers of. The customer seeks a one-stop-shop experience from a brand they can trust. When they find that, not only do they come back for more, but they encourage others to come as well.

Anticipating client need and presenting solutions in a relatable and compelling manner will result in clients feeling personally connected to your brand.

EDUCATION-BASED MARKETING/CONTENT MARKETING

Education-based marketing is a strategy that builds credibility and trust. Sharing your knowledge and expertise offers an opportunity to attract clients to your business. If you become the source of the information your target market seeks, and you sell products or services that offer solutions to their problems or makes their lives better or easier, you will be the obvious choice when they are ready to buy.

Learn the questions on the minds of your target market and answer those questions with your content. You can do this through a Q&A on your website, a blog, or through short videos.

This falls directly in line with content marketing, which is the creation of content specifically designed to attract your target market when shared on social media platforms.

Potential clients don't give you permission to sell them something. They give you permission to add value. They decide when and if they will buy. Through education-based marketing and content marketing you can create brand awareness and attract your target market.

SOCIAL MEDIA MARKETING

Social media marketing is a strategy designed to broaden a brand's reach through content sharing. When developing content that is humorous, thought provoking, and/or emotionally stimulating, it is the business's desire that users will share the content with others. Education- and content-based marketing collateral in the form of images, posts, graphics, videos, and blogs is created and shared on various social media platforms. The business is hopeful that its audience of potential clients/consumers will grow when their content goes "viral."

This is also a marketing strategy for building and maintaining client relationships. Consumers feel personally connected to the business when they relate to the content. Social media marketing is an opportunity to "touch" consumers on a daily basis, putting the brand in the forefront of the consumer's mind.

Plan out your content in advance and determine what platforms you will be posting to. Post regularly and be consistent about doing so. It is also important for a small business to interact as the brand. Don't post and ignore. Follow your own accounts and be sure to respond quickly when users engage. Check your messages regularly, as the modern consumer uses these platforms as if they were an extension of your business.

IN-PERSON NETWORKING

When it comes to a small business, the owner is the star of the show. You *are* your business, and no one can represent it quite like you can. Getting in front of people always pays off. Make a great impression and you will be on the tip of their tongues when they are interacting with others who can benefit from what your business offers.

More than any other reason, a person makes a purchase based on how they feel. Nothing evokes emotional connection like a human interaction. Get out from behind the screen and go connect with others!

MARKETING OPTIONS GALORE

Direct mailers, contest marketing, printed flyers, newsletters, business-to-business collaboration, telemarketing, and free sample marketing all fall under the category of marketing. Do your research and know which strategies will resonate best with the market you seek to attract.

Marketing is an ongoing creative process that will always need your attention. Do not take your eyes off this aspect of your business, even for a moment, as it is fast paced and always changing. You must stay on top of it in order to maintain a constant flow of new clients.

Rule #5: You've Got to Be Found on the Web

Let's talk about Google for a minute. You, me, we are Google's customers. Google wants us to be pleased with the results they offer us when we use them to search for something. They know that we have other options if they return a result that doesn't take us to what we want.

Let's say I want frozen yogurt, which I actually do right now ... So I go to Google and I type in the words, "fro yo near me." Google returns the results and the first one I click on sells frozen yogurt in 26 varieties, 4 blocks away from where I am right now. Perfect. I'm done, I like Google, and I will be eating fro yo within minutes.

But let's say the first result is a broken link. The second is a review of frozen yogurt near me. And the third sells ice cream and not frozen yogurt at all. It won't be long before I leave Google and try something else.

Since Google doesn't want their customers going elsewhere, they have a list of criteria that ranks websites for SERPs (Search Engine Results Pages). The strategy of getting your business to rank high in SERPs is known as SEO or Search Engine Optimization.

KEYWORDS, META DESCRIPTIONS, ALT TAGS, URLS...

Don't panic! SEO can feel overwhelming, but you are a Matriarch and you are totally comfortable using your resources and seeking wise counsel. You also know the value of hiring out what you choose not to do yourself.

If learning and implementing SEO strategies is more time consuming than you can afford to invest, hire it out. Your web designer should be able to optimize your website and advise you on how to continue becoming more and more searchable.

BLOGGING WAY IS ON THE CORNER OF MARKETING ST. AND SEO BLVD

Your business needs a blog and I'll tell you why. We talked about education-based marketing, content marketing, and social media marketing, and a blog is the perfect way to implement them all.

You can choose a topic that a potential consumer might ask about and write a short blog on the topic. Once you do, it becomes a piece of content. Once you share on your social media platforms it becomes part of your social media marketing strategy. But check this out! You can also optimize your blog so that it is searchable for a question a consumer would ask in a Google search!

Imagine if you owned a country store that sells locally grown produce and homemade baked goods. Let's say you know that a common question your target market searches Google for is "When is blueberry season?"

Because you know this is something they ask often, you write a blog titled, "Blueberry Season Starts August 1st!"

Once it's written, you optimize it so that it's searchable on the web, you share it on all of your social media platforms, and before you know it, a blog you wrote three years ago about blueberries drives more traffic to your country store in August of every year than any other piece of marketing collateral! Well done, Marketing Matriarch, well done!

Think of all of the topics you can blog on that will drive traffic to your website, which will drive customers to your country store! The list goes on and on and all you have to do is figure out what your target market wants to know.

Manage Your Time and Follow the Rules

Let's get back to the green portion of your color-coded weekly plan sheet. You now know exactly how many hours per week you will be working on your business. Additionally, you know the five rules of business. Now let me tell you a secret! Every single task involved in growing your business fits into one of those five rules.

A Five Rules of Business Board

Regardless of whether you are just getting your business started or it's in full swing, I want you to create a Five Rules of Business Board. This is either a large dry erase board in your office or a worksheet that you format digitally that allows you to organize your tasks in lists based on the category it belongs to.

For example, the task of filing a form for your taxes would go on a list under Rule #2: It's Got to Be Legal. The task of creating a video about your services would go on a list under Rule #4: Marketing Is a Never-ending Process.

As soon as a task comes to mind, put it in its rightful category on your Five Rules of Business Board. When your workday begins, go to your board and choose a task and get started. As you complete a task, remove it from the list. This board will be a constant reminder of exactly what you need to do during your workday. Even a Matriarch sometimes needs a point of accountability. It will help you manage your time, stay on task, and get your business booming!

As You Add New Products or Services, Take It to the Board!

Let's say your business is adding a new service to its services menu. Start by placing the task of "Add information of the new service to your business plan" in the column for Rule #1: It Starts with a Plan.

Ask yourself what must I do for this new service to become "legal" for my business? Add the tasks of "Have a contract written and purchase insurance" in the column for Rule # 2: It's Got to Be Legal.

Next, consider all of the systems that you will need to create and implement for the new service. List those tasks in the column for Rule # 3: It Takes a Systematic Approach.

Now, plan how you will market this new service. Add each task to the column for Rule #4: Marketing Is a Never-ending Process.

And of course you will want to be found on the web for this new service, so the tasks of "Create web content" and "Optimize for search engine results" will go in the column for Rule # 5: You've Got to Be Found on the Web.

With your color-coded weekly plan sheet and your Five Rules of Business Board, you'll be so empowered that you'll be making time and task management your bitches in no time!

Chapter 8

The Payoff Is Personal

By now, I hope it's clear to you that the underlying message of this book, the essential ingredient, the most consequential factor in becoming a Matriarch, is confidence. I hope you also recognize that the stories I've shared with you, the tools that I've given you, and the "Matriarch Must-Do's" that I've assigned to you, are all designed to help you build that confidence.

You see, if I've learned nothing else in the years I've walked this earth, it's that the confidence I build in one aspect of my life can easily be applied to others, which makes the payoff really personal.

Confidence Can Overcome an Old Message

When I was a little girl, maybe seven years old, there was a TV show for kids. At the end of the show, the host would invite all the kids from the audience to come down and dance to the show's theme song. It was my favorite part and I would get up and dance with those kids right there in my living room. I danced like no one was watching, except, one day, people were watching ...

My parents were in the living room and they started laughing hysterically as I swung my body around the living room without inhibition. I was in my happy place and loving the experience of participating in that dance party. For a moment I thought they were laughing at the pleasure I was having, but I quickly realized that wasn't the case.

Through their laughter, I could hear them say, "She can't hear the beat!" and "I can't believe she can't dance!" They were laughing uncontrollably, and I wasn't sure if I liked the attention they were paying me or if I was completely embarrassed. The music ended, I stopped dancing, and that three-to-four-minute life experience was seemingly over ...

However, my entire life since that moment, every single opportunity to dance that has come my way, has been met by the words, "She can't hear the beat" and "I can't believe she can't dance!" For a long time, I was the girl who sat at the table at the wedding while others danced their asses off and had an amazing night.

Each time it happened, I thought to myself, *How do they hear the beat? I'm tapping my foot to what seems like the beat ... Am I wrong? Why can they dance and I can't? Did they take lessons?* These questions would whip through my mind at 100 miles per hour and I never once had an answer for a single one of them.

Each Step of the Way, My Confidence Grew

Over time, I grew. I made self-esteem lists, I created a huge inventory of "I Don't Suck" evidence, I stopped lying to myself about what I wasn't capable of, I stopped asking others to validate my decisions, I started charging my worth, I crafted myself in a way that reflected my authentic self, and I generated success as an entrepreneur.

It was almost like my confidence had previously shrunk down to the size of a tiny seed. The first step, making that self-esteem list, was like digging a small hole in the huge earth and tucking that seed safely away. The "I Don't Suck List" was like the fertilizer that would provide essential "nutrients" for the seed. Discontinuing the lies was the first rain that would water the seed. The release of the need for validation was the bright sunshine that my seedling would grow toward.

Crafting the best version of myself based on authenticity would become the strong stems that would support all of the flowers I would grow.

And before I knew it, I grew the fiercest, most stunning garden *my* world had ever seen.

One day after having done all of this work, I was at an event and I was asked to dance. And just like that, I said, "Fuck it. Yeah, let's dance!" And you know what happened? I danced! And it was really fun.

All my life I had deprived myself of doing something that was fun because I heard a message when I was seven years old. The message wasn't intended to hurt me, but it stripped me of my confidence nonetheless. And now, because of the confidence I have built, I have freed myself of the chains that held me to the chair at those weddings, kept me from trying new things, and held me back when I longed to move forward. That's the payoff. And it's clearly personal.

Confidence, Meet Systems and Tools

I had done the emotional groundwork to get past a deep and painful wound, and while this particular one was dance related, I can assure you there were many others of far greater significance ... Building my confidence through the challenging yet rewarding work that I've outlined in this book positioned me for tremendous professional success. However, in order to maintain confidence when venturing down an unfamiliar path, we must have exceptional systems and the proper tools or our confidence will waver.

Several years ago, I decided I wanted to lose some weight. I joined a weight loss program that hosted weekly meetings and I quickly learned how to calculate my points and plan my meals. The systems and tools, combined with my confidence, equated to a 60-pound weight loss. Go me!

And then, the company that made the packaged bar that I ate every single morning while losing weight, discontinued the product. I was horrified. It was working perfectly, and I was pissed that they were fucking with the "tools" that were so effective for me. Within two weeks, the weight loss program restructured how "points" were calculated, and the entire system I was using was obliterated.

Now keep in mind, it was working. I was completely satisfied and successful. But when the program changed and I could no longer find that packaged bar that had been my breakfast, I lost confidence in the program and my ability to continue wavered.

The CST Trifecta—Confidence, Systems, and Tools

You can have all of the confidence in the world, but if you have no knowledge of how to build exceptional systems and you don't have the proper tools, it's not gonna work. When it comes to building a business, it's the combination of confidence, systems, and tools that makes the magic happen.

Because a Matriarch is resourceful, once she takes the necessary steps to become confident or increase her level of confidence, she is able to find and create the systems and tools to build the badass business she aspires to. She is confident when researching customer relationship management systems for client management. She is detailed about work flows and sales funnels and her e-mail marketing campaigns are on point. When a Matriarch is able to build a career based on passion and she has the CST Trifecta in place, there's nothing that can stop her. The rewards will come in the form of an overflowing grateful heart and an overflowing ass-kickin' bank account. And that payoff is definitely personal!

Passion: A Strong and Barely Controllable Emotion

When I was about 13 years old I had some experiences. Well, it was actually one experience that I got to have over and over again, and it inspired the passion that lives within me today. My family and I spent many of our weekends in New Jersey at my aunt and uncle's house. I would wake up in the morning and secretly sneak down to the bottom of the stairs, which were just outside the kitchen. In the kitchen at a small table

And that's when I realized … she wasn't trying to find *her* passion. She was trying to borrow mine. She wanted to feel how I felt, she wanted the soulful connections that I am so passionate about developing, but she didn't have the passion for it that I did.

It sucks that she bailed, and I wish her the very best. I also know that if she didn't really care, if she wasn't really trying to find *her best self*, she wouldn't have been so inspired by me being mine.

Inspiration and Motivation

I recently hosted a business class for a group of female entrepreneurs in Connecticut. These women were true Matriarchs in the making; they were all raising families while tending to the never-ending demands of owning a small business. One woman raised her hand to ask a question: "Running a business takes so much work, how do you STAY *so motivated*?"

When I looked at the dozens of women who had gathered together that day to learn how to make their businesses bigger, better, and stronger, I was inspired. Their investment in themselves inspired me. I also find it incredibly fulfilling that I get to play a small role in women's lives as they journey from working mom to badass Matriarch. That feeling is like rocket fuel to me; it inspires me to grow, learn, do better, do more, and work harder at everything I do.

But you and I both know that inspiration isn't enough, right? We know that inspiration is everywhere; it's free for the taking; but motivation – that shit's personal and we have to find it within ourselves if we want the enormous payoff it offers.

So, Let's Get to the "Why"

Now buckle up, cause I'm about to tip a sacred cow here …

All of this bullshit about "finding your why" is exactly that … BULLSHIT. You want to know your why? Why you do the things you do? I'll tell you. It's because you want to and you can. It's that simple. I mean c'mon, you make a hotdog for your kids because you need to feed them. You prepare a feast on Thanksgiving because you want to and you can.

If we could be motivated by outside sources like our children, women wouldn't shoot dope while they were pregnant anymore. And if we could do things to prove to others that we were capable, shame and self-doubt would cease to exist.

All of the gurus out there with this bullshit about finding your why factor are simply sending you on a wild goose chase to find what I know will just be a *temporary* increase in your motivation. It won't last.

The only thing that will truly motivate you enough to transform any difficult-to-change thing in or about your life is your desire to and your ability to. And that's it. Any flowery, butterfly wishing meme or graphic that tells you otherwise should be deleted instantly.

So my answer to the woman's question about how I'm able to stay so motivated is quite simple.

#1—I want to!

#2—I can!

I want to (because the payoff is personal) and I can (because I have the confidence, systems, and tools to do it). I could easily tell you that the inspiration I get from seeing others succeed is my why, but that wouldn't be true. That's certainly fulfilling but it's not WHY I go to work every day.

You and you alone are your WHY. The problem is, if you don't believe you are worthy of the change, you won't do it for yourself. That's where all of this seeking outside sources for your "why" comes from. It's easier to tell you to come up with some beautifully impressive reason for making a monumental change in your life than it is to teach you how to believe you are worthy of it. By the way, there is NO payoff in shifting your focus away from what's broken about you.

So, girl, instead of looking for your why, you're gonna have to look deep inside yourself and take some history-changing actions to get yourself feeling worthy.

FAILURE IS EASIER; DON'T GIVE IN!

If you want to be successful in both life and business, it's going to take hard work. But the thing about hard work that causes people not to do it is that it is HARD. WORK. And that is the exact reason why the payoff is so personal. When you do it, you feel a sense of pride, empowerment, and fulfillment.

But we all know that failure is easier. It takes far less commitment and much less work. And the thing about failure, besides making you *feel* like a failure, is that it's unfulfilling and leaves you unsatisfied, disappointed, and feeling unworthy of success.

I'm gonna make you a promise right now. I promise you that the more you sit and think about how fucked up your life is, the more fucked up it will become. The more you sit in your shit and feel like the world and the people in it have fucked you over and left you emotionally bankrupt, the more miserable you will become.

You gotta do something. You have to accomplish something. I don't care if it's organizing your linen closet or sending that proposal that you've written and rewritten 42 times. DO something. At the end of this day, THIS DAY RIGHT HERE, I want you to have accomplished something ... anything. Girl, you need to look back on this day and feel a sense of worth. That is the payoff. How you feel IS the payoff. You can't get or stay motivated if you don't reap the reward of a personal payoff.

I want to be clear. I'm not coming at you from a place of arrogance. This isn't, "Look at me, I get up every day and xyz and if you don't, you suck." That is NOT what I'm saying here. What I'm saying is I don't want you to hurt anymore. I don't want you to sit in sadness and wait for it to end. I want you to breathe all the way in. And I want you to slowly and mindfully let it go. I want you to lead the life you always wanted, but to do that, YOU have to be the LEADER of it, and I know you're capable of that.

You are a Matriarch and a Matriarch doesn't hope things change; she makes them change!

Maintaining Motivation

Now that you know that the things you do, you do because you want to and you can, we have to talk about the days where you don't want to. The days where you feel tired or lazy or would just rather be doing something else. That IS going to happen as you probably know, and if you succumb to it too often, you can say goodbye to that payoff.

As a business owner, you don't have a boss who will fire you if you're late or over your approved number of days off ... You have to set your schedule and go to work like your boss will be pissed if you called out sick. If you worked for me, would you be a no-show on lazy, tired days or would you be a "do it anyway" kind of girl?

You have to be your own point of accountability and that's not always gonna be easy. But you're not looking for easy, Matriarch. You're looking for a payoff!

PUSH THROUGH WHEN THE EXCITEMENT DIES OUT

In the beginning, desire will lead you, and your excitement will fuel your desire. Each day you will find yourself absorbed in doing what you love and creating a career around it. Your enthusiasm will keep you determined, when things seem difficult, and will help you to move forward as you navigate new waters.

But one day you won't feel excited. You will have settled into a routine where things can begin to feel a little mundane. You may have some frustrating clients or a complication with your bookkeeping. Maybe the owner of the building you're renting isn't on top of issues you've reported, and the business's day-to-day bullshit is dragging you down.

I want you to recognize that as a sign or signal that it is time to expand your knowledge base. A Matriarch never stops seeking inspiration, learning, and trying new things. She also takes tremendous pride in what she's created, so if you stop feeling that pride, it's time to kick things up a notch.

The renewed enthusiasm you will find when you nourish yourself with continuing education in the field where your excitement originated, will motivate you to clean up the straggling details that have robbed you of your enthusiasm.

PUSH THROUGH DURING PERSONAL CRISIS

Ahhh ... personal crisis. Look Matriarch, just because you're doing everything you can to own your power, know your worth, and lead the life you've always wanted, that doesn't mean you get a lifetime pass on personal crisis. It just means you have what it takes to get through it.

You think I don't ever find myself in personal crisis? You think I don't cry? That I don't get so frustrated and pissed off that I want to break things? I cry so hard my eyes swell shut. I fight with my husband, I yell at my kids, I lose my shit when things don't go the way I want them to.

And then somehow, I come to the realization that I'm facing a complication, not a catastrophe. When I find myself in a place like this, typically it's because I am having an amplified reaction to what's going on. I know well enough now to recognize this as a time to pause. To take a small step back and replenish my energy. Extra self-care. A day off. A spa day. A reward for my hard work as a woman, wife, mother, entrepreneur, and person who gives more than she takes.

I come back to the "complication" less aggressive, with less emotion, and with an increased ability to see the other person's perspective, and I'm able to find resolve.

During times of personal crisis, our responsibilities to our businesses do not disappear. So we must compartmentalize tasks by levels of urgency. It is imperative that we get our shit together and get back to work as quickly as possible.

PUSH THROUGH AFTER A FALL

Here's the deal. Shit happens, and sometimes you will fall. You or someone else will do something, say something, or make some big decision on behalf of your business that seems perfectly fine and it will be wrong. Way wrong. You'll feel like there's no coming back from it. You will lose people, or money, or reputation, and you will fall flat on your ass.

You will fall so fucking hard that it will knock the wind out of you, and you will think, in that moment, *I give up*.

Go ahead and think that ... FOR A MOMENT ... and then, snap out of it. Seek wise counsel, do some damage control, wipe your eyes, put some lipstick on, and go back at it. The payoff is personal and, Bitch, you didn't work this hard to go out on a fall.

Pressure Is How Diamonds Are Made

Matriarchs, we are in a strange time in our world. For every message we receive, there is an equal and opposite message in the form of a meme in our Facebook feeds.

These mixed messages can be confusing, but the ones I find most unsettling, most ridiculous, most insulting to women, are the ones that coddle us. The ones that tell us to be satisfied with just brushing our teeth and getting the kids off to school. The ones that tell us to go easy on ourselves. Don't pressure your fragile little self ...

C'mon! Where is the satisfaction in a day where all I did was clean my teeth and open the door so my kids can get on the school bus? I'm all for celebrating life's small victories, but a day where a seven-year-old accomplishes more than I did is no kind of day to be proud of.

I don't know how, but ladies, we are in the midst a "let yourself off the hook movement," and I'm here to give you a big fat fucking reality check. You are not a pussy. You are capable of achieving great things and can meet the expectations you place on yourself.

I want a *daily* payoff, and for me, it comes in the form of feeling accomplished. I can't look back on a day where I anticipated productivity and not feel like shit if all I have to show for it is no cavities and kids with one more day of public school education in them.

Keep in mind, if you *plan* to rest and binge a show on Netflix all day on Sunday after a kick-ass week – and Sunday night rolls around and you accomplished that, you win. Rest is NOT off limits! It's obviously necessary, but it's not random. You don't randomly need to slow down to a sloth's pace for two weeks when you have goals and dreams and aspirations.

So, girl, put a little pressure on yourself and stop letting yourself off the hook. It's not serving you well and you know damn well that you deserve more.

A PROCRASTINATION STRATEGY

Let's say you want to take a day off. You want a pajama day. A lay around, do nothing, scroll social media, eat junk food, watch *Judge Judy* day.

OK, you're a human being; you're capable of making decisions and you're entitled to a day off now and then. You understand consequences and cause and effect, right? So, just before a self-indulgent act of procrastination, ask yourself, *If I do this, will I feel like shit about it later?* If the answer is yes, don't do it! If the answer is no, go for it!

The payoff in life lives in how you feel about how you live it.

A Matriarch Maintains and Protects What She Builds

Because the payoff of your hard work is such a crucial part of the big picture, you must maintain and protect what you've built. What you've built is your confidence, self-esteem, and self-worth, and your life depends on you keeping those things intact.

In business, that means providing exceptional customer service. Staying current on expenses, billing, invoicing, payroll. Maintaining inventory and paying attention to details. It means being honest with yourself about whether or not you are doing your best and, if not, changing that immediately. It is setting goals and achieving them and not making excuses. It's maintaining an impeccable reputation.

Personally, that means living within your budget in a clean and organized space. It means keeping your car clean and staying on top of your finances. It means being in a healthy relationship and only keeping the company of people who respect you and who you respect – including your children.

Your kids leaving dishes out or dirty clothes *next* to the hamper but not *in* the hamper, sends your subconscious a message that you are a peon, one who is beneath those she serves. But wait a minute ... You're not their bitch. You're a fucking Matriarch and you don't peel other people's dirty underwear out of their inside out pants ... Get a grip.

Where is the payoff in this idea of "choosing your battles" with your kids? I don't choose my battles; I set expectations and my children meet them. They respect me and that payoff is extremely personal.

BOUNDARIES AND BARRIERS

There is a crucial difference between boundaries and barriers. When you set boundaries, you're telling your family, friends, and co-workers what kind of behavior is and is not acceptable to you. You're outlining the standards by which you function most comfortably and efficiently. By being clear about those standards, people quickly learn what they can expect from you and what is acceptable to you.

Setting appropriate boundaries prevents others from depleting the energy that you work so hard to generate. It is undeniably easier to put up barriers and shut people out of your life, and ultimately you may have to do that from time to time, but don't miss out on relationships because you didn't clearly define your boundaries.

Make NOT Having These F.E.A.R.S. Your Biggest Fears

You want a personal payoff? You want to feel like the work you do on yourself, your family, and your career is worth it? Focus on making NOT having the following F.E.A.R.S your biggest fears!

F—Fulfillment—Fulfillment is the achievement of something desired, promised, or predicted. It's an external achievement that enables you to say, "I did it!" Think about a child who screams those words. Their eyes light up, they feel a sense of pride, and they learn the valuable lesson that they are capable of achievement. Allow yourself to indulge in that amazing childhood experience by working hard to achieve great things.

E—Experience—Why are we here if not to have life experiences? Personal encounters keep us growing. Boredom is a sign that life is passing you by. Go live it instead. Decide that you will try new things and meet new people. Learn, grow, live, and generate amazing life experiences that keep you inspired to acquire more.

A—Aspiration—Aspiration is the hope or ambition of achieving something. To be ambitious is to have a mental energy that generates a physical energy. When we aspire to achieve something, we set goals and our ambition drives us to work hard to achieve them. We must always aspire to be the best version of ourselves and work toward increasing our energy and staying positive.

R—Respect—Respect is earned by those who conduct themselves with integrity, treat others with dignity, and hold themselves in high regard. When we earn the respect of others, it is a reflection on ourselves: how we've behaved and the actions we've taken. To be respected is the ultimate compliment and earning it is incredibly empowering.

S—Significance—Feeling special in your relationships and through the recognition of your accomplishments is a basic human need. The feeling of significance comes when you are fully present in life's moments: when you positively impact others and add value by being a productive member of society.

Earning and owning these F.E.A.R.S are the personal payoffs to living your best life. They are the culmination of all that you've worked for and they make continuing on in this journey totally worth it.

■ ■ ■

Do yourself a favor. Make your first thought of every day be *Whatever I do with this day, it better be worth sacrificing an entire day of my life for.*

Girl, you can't ever get a day back. You don't get a do over. Once it's gone, it passes you by forever. But recognize this. It *will* become part of the story you tell in the future. In that story is the personal payoff. If you are proud to tell it, it has paid off. Make damn sure that you're writing one that you'll be proud to tell.

Chapter 9

A Matriarch Leaves a Great Legacy

OK, Matriarch, we're talking about eternity here, and we get one shot at this shit, so we better make damn sure we get it right. Your legacy is what you'll be remembered by when you step off this earth and that is some serious shit.

Do you realize what it means? It means that the accumulated days that you call your life here will leave a lasting impression on those who know and love you. Those people will be tasked with the responsibility of keeping your memory alive. Now hear me clear, lady, your truest power is in the words you leave them saying. The words they string together that represent your seconds, minutes, days, months, and years on this planet.

If today was your very last day here, the day you filled your lungs with air and took your final breath, how would the people who know and love you describe you?

Holy shit, right?!?!

You may feel a sense of panic by this realization. I understand that it's a major "ah-ha moment" when you realize that you haven't just been living one day after another but instead a whole life that will leave a taste in the mouths of others. A sweet taste? A sour one? A salty one? What combination of words will be used to describe the life you lived? Is it a sentence? A paragraph? Is it worthy of a monologue?

Your greatest power in all of life is your ability to influence the memory of your own existence. Take that in for a minute. Breath it all the way in. It's probably the most profound thing I've said in this whole fucking book.

What Exactly Is a Legacy?

A legacy is something transmitted by or received from an ancestor or predecessor. It comes in various forms, as will yours, and it is created by the behaviors and decisions you make on your journey through life.

Your daily actions become your habits, your habits become your path, your path becomes your journey, and your journey becomes your legacy. And just in case you're thinking, "I don't want to leave a legacy ...," that's tough shit because you'll leave one whether you like it or not. And since that's how this works, let's make sure you like yours.

Leaving a Legacy Whether You Like It or Not ...

Now I'm going to do my best to write this chapter for you without spilling my tears on the pages of your new favorite book here, but like I said, this shit is heavy. It's really powerful. I mean we're talking next level. So if you're not quite ready, let this one marinate for a while until you've taken some of the other steps we've talked about. I think you've got a little time, but let's not wait too long because the legacy you're going to leave is based on the life you are currently living. That said, once you become intentional about what legacy you want to leave, it will become the road map for every single thing you do for the rest of your life. It's the address you'll punch into your personal GPS that will lead you to your final destination.

I'm going to tell you a little bit about my mom. But keep in mind that in order for me to do this, I'll have to get a little vulnerable. I'm doing this for you, not for me. I'm doing it because you need it, I want you to have it, and it's the clearest way for me to explain this concept.

My Mom, Shari ...

Suddenly my hands are a bit shaky and my insides feel a little warm. There is an uneasiness in my spirit and I'm second guessing every word that I type. BUT, and it's a big but, my inner GPS is taking me down this road, and I trust it. So here goes ...

My mom was strong. She was a force to be reckoned with. She was smart as fuck: well read, a source of great knowledge and creativity. She was artistic, a brilliant wordsmith, and had a tongue of steel that could put anyone in their place. She had a passion and a fire that burned within her. Until she didn't anymore ... I watched my mother, MY mother, the Rock 'n' Roll Doula's mother, surrender to drugs, overeating, and depression. I watched her give up on herself and her children. I watched her fire burn out and I watched her power become engulfed in self-loathing.

My mom left a legacy. Her legacy, the way I remember her, her message to those who knew her and tried to love her was, "I was a badass who simply gave up ... "

The pain that came with this still haunts me to this day, and I find myself heartbroken and furious when I indulge myself in my memories of her. And then the guilt sets in ... But that's probably a whole other book.

My mother didn't have a life destination, a desired life outcome to punch into the GPS. What the fuck am I talking about? That bitch didn't even have a GPS ... I can't help but wonder if this book getting into her hands when she was a young mother, trying to figure things out, could have made a difference.

As her daughter, I struggled to help her hear the messages that I have shared with you. For that reason, I pray that as you read this book, these messages do not fall on deaf ears. In fact, if you are struggling to receive them, let's use Shari, my mom, as our example. Maybe if we do, we can actually rebuild her legacy to be one of redemption. Her story can be a powerful reminder that as long you are still sucking air on this earth, you can find your GPS, and you can decide on what address you want to punch into it. From there, you can follow it to a great destiny and leave a mark – one that the people in your life and the ones you love will be proud to share when you're gone.

A Matriarch Lives an Intentional Life

Almost every day, I think about what people will say about me after I leave this earth. After I'm gone, I don't want people remembering that I complained every time I had to go to the DMV, or that I was afraid of technology, or that I lived vicariously through others. Life doesn't just happen to me; I live it and I live it with intention.

After my wake is over, and the people closest to me kick off their shoes, I want them to talk about how I made them feel when they were with me:

"I always felt bigger, better, and stronger in her presence."

"She loved us with every fiber of her being."

"She inspired me to be my very best."

"She believed in me until I could believe in myself."

"I'm proud of her and of the work she did."

"There was no goal she couldn't reach."

"She overcame every obstacle and lived an authentic life."

That's the legacy I want to leave. I want to be certain that the life I live with intention is recognized as just that: a life lived intentionally. And I take deliberate steps every day to make sure that I'm headed in that direction.

Those words, the ones that I desire to softly hear from another dimension long after I'm gone, have guided me and pushed me forward as I've grown from a woman who cared for her two small children during the day while pulling overnight shifts as a postpartum doula, to the co-founder and CEO of the fastest-growing doula certification organization in the country.

Those words have helped this woman, a woman who at one point lived outside, blossom into a fierce Matriarch whose career as a birth worker and business leader makes other people feel bigger, better, and stronger. I recognize that the beauty of contributing to the empowerment of others is that my own power is not diminished in the process. In fact, it increases.

And now, you, my dear Matriarch, have some work to do. You must begin the process of evaluating your life and the impression it is currently designed to leave. You must ask yourself what memories you are instilling about yourself into the minds of others. If you were a fly on the wall after your death at the first family gathering, what would be said about you?

What stories would be told?

What sentiments would be shared?

What legacy will you leave?

Your legacy is the most important address that you will ever put in your GPS of life, and most people don't even do it. That GPS is where you get your direction, and the support of your inner sanctum will be the voice that says "recalculating" when you venture off your path.

A Matriarch has a vision for her future and beyond it. She has a destiny and if she can't find it, if life kicked her ass too hard for too long, she stops. She decides absolutely no. fucking. more. Not another day of this. She recognizes the micro moments in her life where she has a choice and she stops ignoring them. She begins to hear her own inner voice whisper, *You can do better.* And she stops cranking up the music to drown it out. Instead, she listens. She begins to believe it and she seeks wise counsel to figure out her next move. She remembers that she is resourceful, and she decides that life is too important to waste.

A Matriarch Cultivates an Inner Sanctum

Girl, you can't do this alone, but make no mistake, it doesn't take a village. You certainly don't need the village idiot helping you. What it takes is a carefully and deliberately curated small group of other women who deeply love and respect you and who truly understand your desired life destination. This is your most intimate circle and it is often where you turn for wise counsel surrounding your most personal life matters.

You need women who make you feel so comfortable and supported that you can reach up, pull down that big steel zipper that starts at your forehead and ends at the tip of your toes, and open yourself to speak freely from your soul.

These women are your inner sanctum. These women are visionaries. They are fun. They are full of life. They are not competing with you or jealous of you. They are as excited when something good happens for you as if it happened to them too.

When you're facing something hard, whether it's in business or with your kids or inside your body, the women in your inner sanctum are wise and full of words that breathe hope into your lungs. I can't help but think what a difference having a fierce, loyal, and loving inner sanctum would have made for my mom ...

Your inner sanctum "gets you," and they're on board for the ride to your final destination. They are fully aware of the legacy you intend to leave, and they plan to keep your memory alive long after you're gone. And because they do, they also hold you accountable to it.

When two of the women in my inner sanctum said to me, "Mom, your entire last year can be described in these three sentences."

"I'm working, I'll call you back."

"I'm picking up sushi."

"I'm at the grocery store."

I knew I had ventured off my path, and their nonjudgmental "nudge" became the voice in my GPS that said, "Recalculating." I had gotten caught up in work and lost any and all sense of balance. Clearly my legacy plans got temporarily sidetracked.

Hearing my daughters share those insightful words in a way that wasn't critical of me woke me up. It got me back on track, and while there had been so many signs along the way that said, "Caution turn back," hearing it without condemnation helped me realize I had made a wrong turn.

A Matriarch Gives and Takes

A Matriarch nurtures the women in her inner sanctum giving them the love, wisdom, and support they need as well.

She engages them in conversations about the legacies they plan to leave because she recognizes how significant they are and she does not want their lives to be lived in vain. They matter to her and to others now and forever, and she wants the world to remember them for eternity.

Regardless of her full life and grueling schedule, she makes time for these relationships that she holds sacred. She values these women most, for she knows there are few in life that she is able to both give to *and* take from equally. These bonds are strong, and they make the Matriarch even stronger. (*Shout out to my bitches! You know who you are!*)

A Matriarch Rocks Out to Her Own Soundtrack

In business you have a mission statement: an expression, made by you as its leader of the desires and intent of your organization. It is a crucial part of creating your company's identity and conveying it to your employees and customers. And in life, we have missions, too. They are how we express what is important to us and what our desires are. They convey our current (it often changes over time) "identity" to our loved ones and acquaintances.

We are moms and Girl Scout leaders; we are Pampered Chef ladies for a season; and then maybe we are photographers for a time. We are the church nursery volunteers and the PTO presidents. We are employees who later become entrepreneurs. Whatever it is that we are doing is a mission, and throughout life our missions change. What does not and should not change if we are to be true Matriarchs who leave a great legacy is the soundtrack of our lives. This unfortunately is where I watched my mother's future legacy crumble. Her soundtrack, which once featured titles like, "Life Is Ours, We Live it Our Way" and "If it Feels Good, Do it" faded out and were replaced by titles that included "I Surrender" and "It Doesn't Even Matter …"

I chose a soundtrack as a metaphor for your life message because the power of music to move a human spirit cannot be overstated. I was 16 years old, and when Ronnie James Dio belted out the lyrics to "Stand Up and Shout," in those 3 minutes and 16 seconds, I was the driver; I owned the road, I was the fire, and I would explode!

In the doula industry I am known as the Rock 'n' Roll Doula, whose battle cry is "Charge your worth!" That would definitely be a song on my life's soundtrack, which is titled "Women, Own Your Power." Every battle cry I raise, every song I sing, every message I speak is some variation of that title.

What is the title of your soundtrack? What is the message you bring to every season and every mission of your life that tells the story of the legacy you will leave?

A Matriarch Knows Her Language Is Her Legacy

When my pregnant client looked me in the eye after 31 hours of labor feeling defeated, in sheer exhaustion, and whispered, "I can't do this anymore." I didn't say, "I know." I said, "Dig deeper. You have the strength within you. Find it and bring it here now!" She felt bigger, better, and stronger in my presence.

You may not be pushing a baby out or helping someone else do it, but the language you use when talking to yourself and others *will* become part of your legacy. Using language that positions you and those around you for success generates positive energy. And positive energy now makes for a positive legacy later.

Are you a complainer? Do you find fault? What is the clearest message you're conveying? Is it that everyone is an asshole? Is it that you're helpless, hopeless, and miserable? Is it that you're scattered and you're being pulled in every different direction?

Is it that ...

YOU TRIED?

YOU COULDN'T?

YOU WERE TOO BUSY?

YOU HAD NO CHOICE?

I'm not saying we don't all have obstacles that knock us on our ass and that we have to learn to overcome, but what I'm asking you is, do these things define you? Do they define the message you are leaving behind? Has the lens of your life been so focused on these problems that you risk conveying a nondeliberate message as your legacy?

A Matriarch Switches Gears When Necessary

Look, we cannot allow the stories of our past to continue to dictate our future. I grew up at a time where a common parenting philosophy was "Children should be seen and not heard." Imagine how difficult it is to "find your voice" when you're raised to believe you shouldn't even have one.

I mean, there wasn't some magical day where my parents sat me down and said, "OK, you're old enough now to be seen and heard. Welcome! You look great and we want to hear everything you've been thinking for all these years ..."

Add to that, the theme of *my* childhood, which was ... "Don't get your hopes up ..." and you have the perfect recipe for low self-esteem and a "why bother" attitude.

I remember one day walking into school, I must have been about 10 years old. We were told about a contest where the prize was a bicycle. A brand-new bicycle! Not like the bikes we had that were too small for us and had no brakes, whose handlebars and seat came from a bike left on the curb for trash pickup.

It was an essay writing contest. I can't recall what the topic of the essay was to be or any details about that part at all, but I remember being handed a piece of paper, it was called a "ditto sheet" back then, and it outlined the contest rules.

As I was running down the hill from the school that day to our apartment, I remember holding that ditto sheet in my hand and the excitement that I would burst through the door with. I remember how badly I wanted that bicycle. I also remember believing without a shadow of a doubt, that I would be the winner. I don't know why I believed that, but I could see it so clearly: the big announcement of ME as that bike's new owner. I could see my classmates applauding and cheering for me. I could feel the wind in my face as I imagined peddling that bike all over town, and then, I opened the door. The house was dark.

The curtains were closed. My mom was in a valium-induced "peace" on the couch.

As I burst into the apartment I shouted, "Mom, mom! Guess what?! I'm gonna win a bicycle!!! I'm gonna write an essay and enter a contest, and I'm gonna win a BICYCLE!"

And that's when she lifted her head, drowsily opened one eye, and said the words that shattered my dream, destroyed my confidence, and made me want to stop trying: "Don't get your hopes up. Everyone thinks they're gonna win."

What I heard my mother say was, "You're not good enough, and no essay that you can write will win you that bicycle."

The words she spoke instantly became my reality. So much so, that I didn't write an essay, I didn't enter the contest, and I sure as hell didn't win that bicycle. I struggled for a long time when it came to writing. I was insecure and I believed I was a bad student and a slow learner.

But like I said, we can't let the stories of our past dictate our future, and it's never too late to turn things around. It may have taken me four decades to erase the negative message I got that day, but now I'm writing a book, mother fuckers! How's that for changing history and leaving a legacy you're proud of?!

Live Like a Matriarch and Leave a Legacy Worthy of a Matriarch!

Girl, I swear, it's not too late to redirect the narrative of your life. It's not too late to start family traditions that can be passed down from generation to generation. It's not too late to love more passionately, to live more deliberately, or to step out of your comfort zone and take a risk. You are a Matriarch, and the sooner you begin to believe it, the sooner you will own your power, know your worth, live the life you've always wanted, and leave a kick-ass legacy in your place.

You see, in your world, when you take on your rightful role as a Matriarch, it will allow you to build and foster the life you've always dreamed of living. One where you are respected because you are fair, honest, committed, and morally worthy of it. One where you protect and nourish your people. Where you inspire and show kindness. Where your composure and ability to provide order benefits all. And where your partner, your inner sanctum, and your wise counsel sit with you lovingly at the round table of decision making.

My kids need me to be a Matriarch, and FYI, yours do too. We are raising the next generation of women (and men) and we must be deliberate about how we do it. We must lead by example. Our daughters will carry on our legacies and they will build upon them with the strengths they find within themselves. They will also one day become Matriarchs, and your legacy will live forever in their hearts. It will reveal itself in their words, their success, their ability to know their worth, and their dedication to owning their power. The traditions they hold dear will honor you and keep your legacy alive. You, my friend, will not be forgotten.

About the Author

Not your average entrepreneur and CEO of a multi-million dollar start up. **Randy Patterson** leads with purpose and compassion, reducing fear and instilling strength in all who make her acquaintance. Her passion for supporting women is only equaled by her desire for personal growth and success. She has built an empire, coaching women in both the birth and business spheres, giving them the confidence, systems, and tools to own their power, know their worth, and lead the lives they always wanted.

Randy speaks in blatant truths that emancipate, challenge, and motivate audiences without effort. She has penned and published several full course curricula for birth workers, created business resources and templates that have contributed to the success of others, and has a blog prowess that keeps her closely involved with her growing global membership.

With attention-commanding looks and a powerful stage presence, Randy wows live audiences with a variety of topics relating to birth and parenting; business development; sales and marketing; and personal topics such as self-esteem, confidence, and relationships. As an international speaker, Randy connects on a deep level with each individual, whether in small intimate settings or center stage with groups of 2,500+. Audiences leave feeling affirmed, inspired, and revived.

Randy Patterson represents the badass within all of us. Unrelenting, unshakeable, and unapologetic: yet soft, approachable, and relatable. Born to hippie bikers, her foundation was built on fighting the establishment and going against the grain. As a heavy metal headbanging teenager slinging records at her family's legendary record store, she was always ahead of the curve. Fighting tooth and nail through homelessness and addiction to earn her space, it was her tenacious spirit that got her here, and her "nothing can stop me" attitude that keeps her going.

Along the way, life lessons never stop coming, and she never stops sharing them with the tens of thousands of clients, friends, fans, and followers that she engages with through various social media platforms. Because she believes that women are valuable and the work they do is credible, the battle cry of the Rock 'n' Roll Doula is above all else, "Charge Your Worth!"

Randy believes that prioritizing herself as a woman first, wife second, and mother third enables unbreakable bonds with self, partner, and family. Her truest calling has always been in raising and empowering her daughters: Erica, 27 and Tyler, 23. Together with her incredibly supportive and loving husband of 30 years, Jerry Patterson, they worked tirelessly to instill self-worth, purpose, and esteem in their children and now fully enjoy the fruit of that labor.

■ ■ ■

To contact Randy Patterson for the purpose of speaking at your next event, elevating your business, motivating your team, private consulting services, or press inquiries, you can find her kicking ass over at www.randypattersononline.com. Or e-mail her at therocknrolldoula@gmail.com

Index

Acknowledgment of setbacks, 33–34
Aesthetic, brand, 101–104
Aspiration, 145
Authenticity, 37, 103
  branding and, 97–101

Back end of the I'm Too Busy lie, 49–50
Benefits-risks-alternatives (BRA)
    decision-making, 70–71
Blakely, Sarah, 91
Blatant "I'll Try" lie, 43–44
Blogging, 127–128
Boundaries and barriers, healthy, 144
Branding
  aesthetic of, 101–104
  based on compliments you'd like to
    receive, 101
  based on passions, 99
  based on principles you stand for and
    believe in, 100
  based on what matters most, 98
  based on what other people should
    feel after spending in your
    presence, 99–100
  based on what worries you, 99
  based on your authentic self, 97–101
  beliefs and principles to fight for and,
    100–101
  brand-shaping role of Matriarchs
    and, 19
  of a carefully crafted Matriarch
    business, 108–111
  defined, 93
  discovery session for, 98
  family, 105–106
  finding the starting point for, 106–108
  friendship and, 100
  how NOT to find yourself and,
    103–104
  by Nike, 94
  and people as their own brands,
    94–96
  personal style guide and, 104–105

  target markets and, 109–111
  voice and, 102–103
  where you see yourself in 10 years
    and, 100
  working for free becoming part
    of your, 76
Business banking, 121
Business plans, 119–120

CEO role inventory, 28
Check cashing businesses, 14
Choice, 55–56
"Chump feelings," 56
Communities, giving back to, 89–90
Compliments, accepting, 34, 101
Conceit, 34
Confidence, 63–67
  being prepared and, 66
  facing and conquering fears and, 66
  looking like you have, 65
  overcoming an old message with,
    131–133
  positive self-talk for, 66–67
  recognizing insecurity as bully and, 66
  setting and attaining small achievable
    weekly goals for, 67
  systems and tools for increasing,
    133–134
  trusting someone who believes in you
    for, 67
Content marketing, 124–125
Contracts, 121–122
Co-signers, 59, 60, 61–62
  co-signing your agenda or her own,
    62–63
Culture, family, 21–22

Decision-making, 29
  history-changing actions, 30–32
  living each day to the fullest and,
    38–39
  owning the, 57–71
  personality styles of, 68–69

Decision-making (*contd.*)
  protecting your dreams with your life
      and, 39–40
  steps in, 67–71
  tallying successes, not failures and,
      32–34
  working through struggles with, 70–71
  writing the story of you and, 35–37
Decisions, owning one's, 57–59
  confidence and, 63–67
  co-signers and (*See* Co-signers)
  steps in, 67–71
  wise counsel and, 59–62
Discovery sessions, 98
Dreams, protecting your, 39–40
Duchant, Charles, 105–106
Duchant, Marie, 105–106

Education-based marketing, 124–125
Escape clause "I'll Try" lie, 44
Excitement, pushing through in times
      of less, 140–141
Executive summary, business plan, 120
Experiences, value of new, 145

Facebook, 64–65, 114
Failures, pushing through after, 141–142
Families
  branding of, 105–106
  mission of, 21
  normal, 4–5
  taking care of each other, 21–22
  who love, but don't care for, their
      children, 3–4
Fear, 32, 66
  of being judged, 85
  facing and conquering, 82–91
  imposter syndrome, 84
  making NOT having F.E.A.R.S. your
      biggest, 144–145
  of the unknown, 86–87
Fearless leader role, 22–24
Five Rules of Business Board, 128–129
Free work. *See* Working for free
Friendship, 100
Front end of the I'm Too Busy lie, 47–49
Fulfillment, 144–145

Give and take, 152–153
Giving back to the community, 89–90

Goals list, 8
Google, 126–127
Growing pains in business, 118–119
Gut feelings, 68

History-changing actions, 30–32
  for time management, 115–117
Homelessness, 10–12
Hurting
  others, 47
  of self, 46–47

I Can't Do One More Thing feeling, 53
I Can't Explain feeling, 54
I Can't Keep Going feeling, 53
I Can't lie, 50–55
I Can't Meet the Need feeling, 53–54
"I Can't," overcoming, 54–55
I Don't Know How lie, 51
"I Don't Like the People" category, 48
"I Don't Suck List," 14, 15, 23
"I Don't Want to Do It" category, 48
I Don't Want To feeling, 52
I Give Up feeling, 52–53
I Had No Choice lie, 55–56
I Have No Self-Control feeling, 53
I'll Try lie, 43–45
Imposter syndrome, 84
I'm Too Busy lie, 45–50
  back end of, 49–50
  front end of, 47–49
Inner sanctum, cultivation of, 151–152
In-person networking, 125–126
Insecurity as a bully, 66
Inspiration, 52, 137–139
Instagram, 114
Insurance, business, 122
Intentional living, 150–151
Internet presence, 126–128
"It's Not Important to You" category,
      47–48
It's Too Hard lie, 51–52
"I Won't Enjoy It" category, 49

Judgment, fear of, 85

Legacy, 147
  defined, 148
  give and take and, 152–153
  inner sanctum and, 151–152

intentional life and, 150–151
language as, 154–155
left whether you like it or
    not, 148
living like a Matriarch and leaving a
    worthy, 156–157
of Randy Patterson's mother, 149
rocking out to your own soundtrack
    and, 153–154
switching gears when necessary and,
    155–156
Legal structure for businesses, 121–123
Lies, big. *See* Self-deception
Living each day to the fullest, 38–39
Loved, but not cared for, persons,
    3–4
Luxuries as not necessities, 88–89

Madonna, 91
Mangano, Joy, 91
Marketing, 124–126
Matriarch(s), 1–2
    branding of (*See* Branding)
    choosing her own soundtrack,
        153–154
    cultivating an inner sanctum, 151–152
    description of, 2–3
    give and take by, 152–153
    knowing her language is her legacy,
        154–155
    legacies left by, 147–157
    living intentional lives, 150–151
    maintaining and protecting what she
        builds, 143–144
    in normal families, 3–4
    owning her decisions, 57–71
    partners of, 27–28
    Randy Patterson as, 7–8
    revolutionizing their fields and facing
        their fears, 82–91
    roles and responsibilities of, 18–27
    self-deception and (*See*
        Self-deception)
    switching gears when necessary,
        155–156
    time management by, 114–117
Mental alarms, 56
Mindful language, 56
Mission statements, 153
    family, 21

Motivation
    inspiration and, 137–139
    maintaining, 140–142
Moving on from setbacks, 33–34

Necessities versus luxuries, 88–89
Nike, 94
Normal families, 4–5

Operations manuals, 123
Others, hurting of, 47
Overthinkers, 69

Passion, 99, 134–137
Patterson, Jerry, 10–12, 15–16
    marriage to Randy, 16
    move back to New York, 17–18
    as President of the Board of Directors,
        27–28
Patterson, Randy
    appearance of "wise counsel" for, 6–7
    becomes a cosmetologist, 16
    children of, 16, 18, 20–21
    craving for "normal" in, 4–5
    first business of, 17–18
    first meeting with, 15
    as homeless, but not helpless, 10–12
    legacy left by mother of, 149
    as a loved, but not cared for, child,
        3–4
    low self-esteem of, 1–2
    marriage to Jerry, 16
    as a Matriarch, 7–8
    move back to New York, 17–18
    second business of, 18–19
    truth moment of, 5–6
    on using your resources to get what
        you want, 12–14
Personal crisis, pushing through
    during, 141
Personal style guides, 104–105
Pinterest, 114
Planning and tracking of your hours, 115
Plans, business, 119–120
Power, personal, 2, 41, 148
    to choose, 55–56
PR director role, 24–26
Pressure, making positive use of,
    142–143
Problem solving role, 23–24

Procrastination, strategy for combating, 143
Protecting your dreams with your life, 39–40

Random acts of kindness, 90
Relationship-based marketing, 124
Research and evidence decision-makers, 69
Respect, 145
Rest, importance of, 142–143
Roles and responsibilities of the Matriarch, 18–19
   creating the culture, 21–22
   defining values, 20–21
   fearless leader, 22–24
   PR director, 24–26
   shaping the brand, 19
   solving problems, 23–24
   stating the mission, 21
   success manager, 26–27
   vision caster, 19

Search Engine Optimization (SEO), 127–128
Security minded decision makers, 68–69
Self-control, 40
Self-deception, 41–43
   I Can't lie, 50–55
   I Had No Choice lie, 55–56
   I'll Try lie, 43–45
   I'm Too Busy lie, 45–50
Self-esteem, 2, 8–10, 29–30, 39
   in persons loved, but not cared for, 3–4
   truth moments and, 5–6
   wise counsel and, 6–7.
      See also Confidence
Self-Esteem List, 8
Self-hurt, 46–47
Self-talk, 63–64, 66–67
Setbacks, acknowledgment of, 33–34
Shakespeare, William, 64
Shaping the brand role, 19
Significance, 145
Social acceptance decision-makers, 68
Social media, 36–37
   marketing on, 125
   as a time-waster, 114–115

Soft "I'll Try" lie, 44
Story, crafting a personal success, 35–37
Success manager role, 26–27
Systematic approach to business, 123

Taking oneself seriously, 90–91
Tallying of successes, not failures, 32–34
Target markets, 109–111
Taxes, business, 122–123
Time management, 114–117
   history-changing action for, 115–117
"Too Invasive" category, 48
Trust, 67, 118
Truth moments, 5–6
Truth-telling, 56

Unknown, fear of, 86–87

Validation, 58–59. *See also* Co-signers
Values, defining, 20–21
Vision caster role, 19
Voice, 97, 102–103

Websites, 126–128
Winfrey, Oprah, 19, 27
Wise counsel, 6–7
   need for, 59–62
   painting the big picture without an agenda, 63
Working for free, 73–75
   becoming part of your brand message, 76
   being "in training" as excuse for, 81
   causing people to expect others to work for free as well, 79–80
   destroying your industry, 78–79
   as a family sacrifice, 81–82
   making another women's career your hobby, 80–81
   not leading to paid work, 77–78
   problems with, 75–82
   stigma attached to, 76–77
   and understanding what "I can't pay your fee" really means, 87–88

YouTube, 37

Zappos, 19